STRIPLATE PIECING

Piecing Circle Designs with Speed and Accuracy

STRIPLATE PIECING

Piecing Circle Designs with Speed and Accuracy

Debra Wagner

American Quilter's Society

P. O. Box 3290 • Paducah, KY 42002-3290

The following products were used to make the samples for this book:

Cotton Classic® Batting by Fairfield Processing was used in all the quilted samples.

Dual Duty® Extra Fine thread by Coats and Clark® was used for piecing and quilting.

Softouch® scissors and rotary cutter by Fiskar® were used to cut all the strips and pieces.

Library of Congress Cataloging-in-Publication Data

Wagner, Debra.
    Striplate piecing : piecing circle designs with speed and accuracy
    / Debra Wagner.
        p.   cm.
    Includes bibliographical references (p. 166).
    ISBN 0-89145-821-2 : $24.95
    1. Strip quilting.   2. Machine quilting--Patterns.   3.Cutting.
I Title.
TT835.W3318   1994
746.46--dc20

                                                94--36355
                                                CIP

Additional copies of this book may be ordered from:

American Quilter's Society
P.O. Box 3290
Paducah, KY 42002-3290
@24.95. Add $1.00 for postage and handling.

Copyright: 1994, Debra Wagner

Dedication

I would like to dedicate this book to my parents, Wes and Esther, for their encouragement and support. They instilled in me the joy of questions and the love of looking for the answers.

My deepest thanks to those many authors and quilters who have so generously, if unknowingly, shared their talents with me. No idea is formed in a vacuum; their work and books gave me a solid foundation and the encouragement to see possibilities.

Jinny Beyer, Anita Hallock, Mary Hickey, Nancy J. Martin, Judy Mathieson, Marsha McCloskey, and Hettie Risinger.

In particular, I want to thank Nancy Crow, for allowing us a look into her studio and work in her book *Nancy Crow: Quilts and Influences*; her work is challenging, complex, and awe inspiring.

I also want to especially thank Barbara Johannah, an innovator in strip piecing and a myriad of other quilting techniques, who is a genius at seeing the obvious and then kindly and patiently pointing it out to the rest of us.

Contents

Foreword

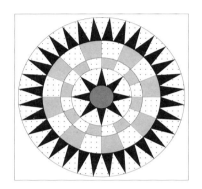

Fig. 1-1. Georgetown Circle.

Fig. 1-2. Pickle Dish.

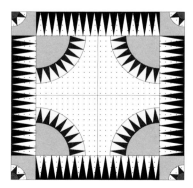

Fig. 1-3. New York Beauty Variation or Rocky Mountain Road.

For every quiltmaker there is a group of patterns that hold a special fascination. For some it may be stars, triangles, or perhaps hexagons. For me the most interesting and challenging patterns are circle designs like Sunflowers, Sunbursts, and Wedding Rings with their innumerable variations. The complex *blend* of long thin points, tiny pieces, and curved edges sparkle like cut crystal.

Traditional piecing methods require handling minute individual pieces. During sewing, these tiny slivers of fabric shift under the presser foot. The results can be blocks that won't fit together or circles that refuse to lie flat. After my initial attempt, I realized there must be a simpler way to approach these patterns. In the process of learning to draft and make these patterns, I came to realize that the technical revolution in quilting had skipped these designs.

Many of the books and patterns I turned to for help advocated hand piecing and hand cutting, with nary a word about the rotary cutter or strip piecing. The general rule was, these complex pieced curves can't be strip cut or sewn. Armed with my rotary cutter and rulers I plunged ahead, seeking a way to blend strip piecing and curved pieces. The result is striplate piecing.

The word *striplate* is a combination of *strip and template*. As a technique, "striplate piecing" combines the speed and ease of strip piecing, plus the accuracy of template piecing. Striplate piecing offers the best of all worlds. It simplifies the cutting of many complex patterns. The piecing is easier and faster than traditional methods. Most surprising of all, the matching points are reduced to simple matches that guarantee super accurate points and true circles!

Welcome to the world of striplate piecing. This book is a primer in the techniques. The patterns are given in order of difficulty, with each new chapter building on the skills of the previous chapter. In completing these quilts and writing this book I have come to realize that I have merely scratched the surface of striplate piecing. It is my hope that the techniques and patterns will provide other quilters with a stepping stone into new and challenging areas of quilt design.

Introduction:

WHAT IS STRIPLATE PIECING?

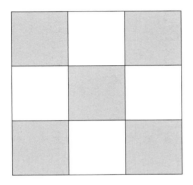

Fig. 2-1. Nine-Patch block.

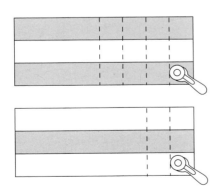

Fig. 2-2. Sew and cut strips into units.

Striplate is the name I have given to my techniques that combine strip piecing with template-cut pieces. It is based on three existing strip piecing methods: basic Nine-Patch, bias-cut squares, and the quick-cut Lone Star. Because of the popularity of these methods I will assume you are familiar with them and I explain them only briefly. If you have a specific question, please refer to resources listed in the bibliography.

The most basic form of strip piecing is the Nine-Patch. *(Fig. 2-1)* The block contains nine identical squares. Each square could be cut and sewn individually, but by changing our focus, the block could be seen as three units of three squares. *(Fig. 2-2)* To make the units, stitch together long strips *(Fig. 2-3)*, and then cut the strips into units. Join the three units to make the block.

The quick-cut Lone Star method *(Fig. 2-4)* involves using rotary cutting to cut multiple complex pieces without a template. It is based on the premise that the Lone Star, much like the Nine-Patch, is in reality composed of rows of pieces rather than individual diamonds, and that the rows are in a repeating pattern. This shift in "seeing" the pattern allows the use of strip piecing methods. At a glance, the steps are:

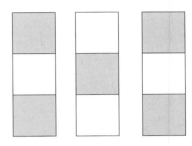

Fig. 2-3. Three units of three squares each.

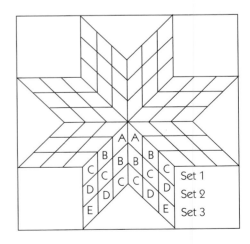

Fig. 2-4.

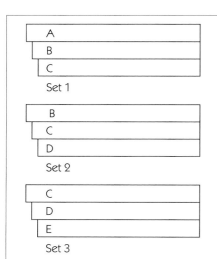

A
B
C

Set 1

B
C
D

Set 2

C
D
E

Set 3

Fig. 2-5.

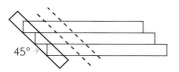

45°

Fig. 2-6.

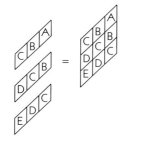

Fig. 2-7.

- Cut the number and correct color of strips needed for each row of diamonds.
- Arrange and sew the strips together to make a stripped fabric unit. *(Fig. 2-5)* Make a fabric unit for each row of diamonds.
- Cut the units into 45° strips. *(Fig. 2-6)*
- Arrange the 45° strips to form the star point and stitch them together. *(Fig. 2-7)*

For bias-cut squares, templates and strip piecing are used to cut two-color squares. Marsha McCloskey introduced me to this ingenious and accurate method of piecing. In its most elementary steps:

- Cut bias strips from two contrasting colors of fabric. *(Fig. 2-8)*
- Sew the strips together to form a stripped unit of fabric.
- Using a plastic template of the square, line up the diagonal line on the template with the seam line of the stripped unit. *(Fig. 2-9)* Trace the square on the wrong side of the fabric.
- Cut the pieces out with scissors. *(Fig. 2-10)*

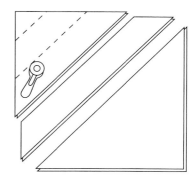

Fig. 2-8. Cut straight strips from bias edge.

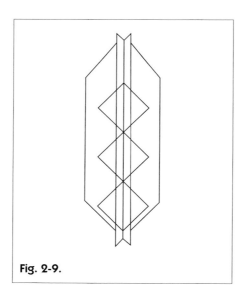

Fig. 2-9.

Fig. 2-10.

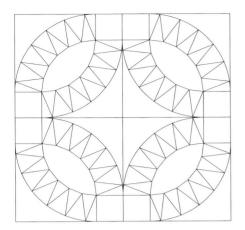

Fig. 2-11. Squashed Pickle Dish.

These three strip piecing methods share five common principles.

- Rotary cut strips are more accurate than hand cut pieces.
- The fewer the pieces the faster and easier the block is to sew.
- As the number of pieces in a block increases, so does the chance for error. Combining pieces and cutting them as a unit minimizes mistakes. I call this the "sew first, cut second" rule of strip piecing.
- Any two pieces with a shared straight edge can be strip pieced to make a single unit.
- Strip piecing can also be applied to multiple pattern pieces with parallel edges. Squares, rectangles, and diamonds are all suitable for strip piecing.

The key is to apply the common principles to circle based designs. A simple application would be the Double Wedding Ring variation, Pickle Dish. *(Fig. 2-11)* There are a number of rotary templates to quick cut the basic Double Wedding Ring. The snag with Pickle Dish is the triangle pieced arcs, every piece in the arc has to be hand drawn and cut. But, by combining two triangles *(Fig. 2-12)* into a strip piecing unit you reduce the number of pieces by one half.

A slightly more complex pattern would be Kansas Sunflower. *(Fig. 2-13)* An average Sunflower has 12 points and three layers of pieces. Including the center and corners, a single block would total about 40 pieces. Traditionally that would mean handling 40 individual pieces. Instead, think of the block as a curved Nine Patch. Remember, any piece with parallel edges can be strip pieced and the diamond fits that description. By strip piecing and cutting the three pieces in a unit *(Fig. 2-14)*, you reduce the number of individual pieces in a block to 17. In addition,

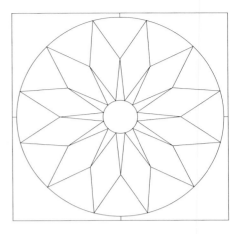

Fig. 2-13. Kansas Sunflower.

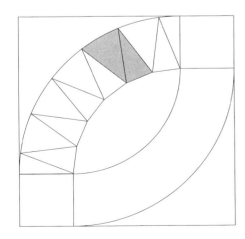

Fig. 2-12.

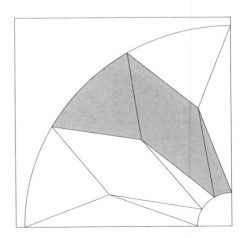

Fig. 2-14.

Fig. 2-15. Sunny Splendor.

these units are extremely accurate and easy to piece.

Why stop there? Even more complex designs can be accomplished by using the idea of the quick cut Lone Star. An 18 point Sunflower with five layers has 95 individual pieces. *(Fig. 2-15)* It is possible to strip cut five pieces in one unit. That reduces the 95 pieces to 23! *(Fig. 2-16)*

Have I piqued your interest? The following chapters give step-by-step directions and explanations of all my methods. As you use this book keep in mind that striplate piecing is based on two simple ideas: *Never* cut any more pieces than absolutely necessary, and, whenever possible, sew first, cut second.

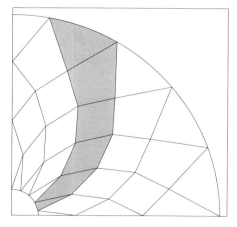

Fig. 2-16.

General Techniques

FABRIC SELECTION

I suggest 100% cotton broadcloth for your first attempt at striplate piecing. Cotton has numerous advantages. It is readily available in a breathtaking array of colors and prints. It is the simplest of fibers to sew, it cuts easily, and it marks clearly. Cotton is easy to care for; it can be machine washed to completely remove any trace of markers. It can be pressed without your worrying about scorching or melting. The pieces hold a crease and maintain their shape. Best of all, small irregularities in stitching can be eased or stretched to insure the finished block is flat. I am not discouraging the use of less traditional fabrics, but, they may be more difficult for the intermediate quilter to handle. Metallics, silks, or cotton blends are suitable for striplate methods and they add sparkle and interest to contemporary quilts.

There are many factors to consider in choosing fabrics. The three basic components are color, scale, and contrast. Looking at quilts, antique or modern, can give you insight into how other quilters use these fabric components. In researching antique quilts for the patterns in this book I was struck by the fabric choices. In almost every case the quilts were solid colored fabrics or small prints. Often the quilts were only two colored, white and red, white and navy, or a large range of dark tones (gold, green, red, blues, and browns) on cream or beige backgrounds. The large light colored areas of background provided a frame for the complex piecing and could be filled with detailed quilting patterns. The choice of fabric indicated these quilts were not scrap quilts. The large amount of matching yardage suggests the fabric was specially chosen and purchased (or dyed) for the pattern. These quilts were "best" quilts, used to feature the skill of the maker. The Spartan use of color and print was a calculated decision. The quilter knew the graphic nature of the pattern depended on form. This may be a radical change for many contemporary quilters. The current selection of beautiful prints can make solid colors or tiny prints look flat and boring. But showing these complex patterns to their best advantage may require modification in the fabric selection process. We need to look at each fabric component individually. The place to begin is with contrast, which can vary greatly, (Fig. 3-1, 3-2).

Contrast refers to the differing amounts of light or dark in fabric. Black

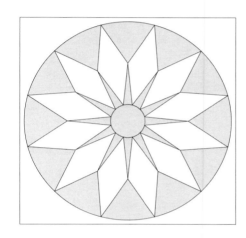

Fig. 3-1.

Fig. 3-2.

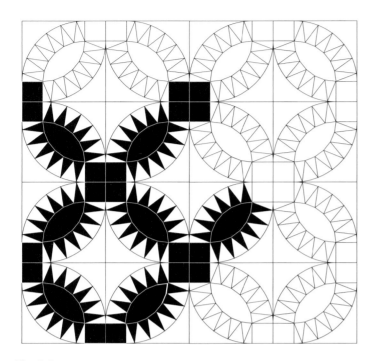

Fig. 3-3.

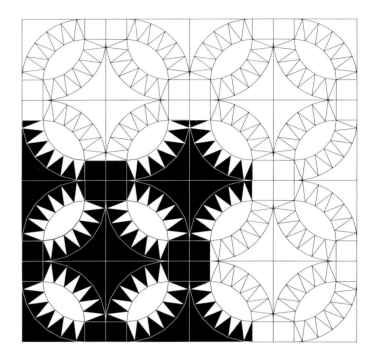

Fig. 3-4.

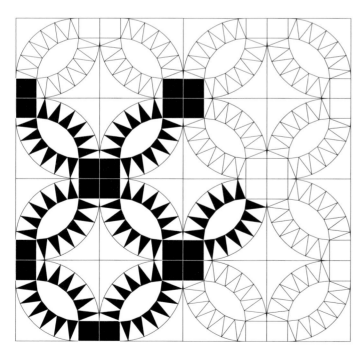

Fig. 3-5.

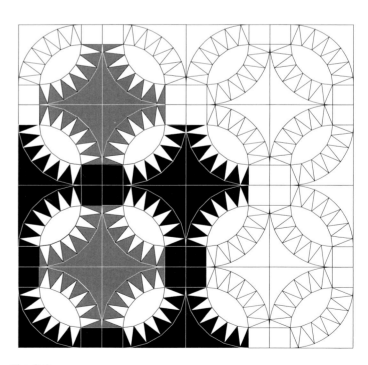

Fig. 3-6.

and white photography is a study in contrast. Without knowing the exact colors, you can delineate features by varying shades of gray. The greater the difference in contrast, the clearer the features. For example, a stark contrast like a black and white pieced quilt is almost shocking and highly visible. It shows every piece and every error. In comparison, low contrast colors like pastel pink and cream may look like a single color from a distance. The low contrast conceals both the piecing and the errors. You can use this effect to your advantage.

Manipulating the contrast between pieces in a block can radically change its appearance. Look at illustrations *3-3* through *3-6*. The blocks are identically pieced, but the contrast between pieces has been changed. Carefully used, contrast can emphasize the piecing and design elements. In illustrations *3-7* through *3-10*, notice what happens when the background fabric is included in the intricate portions of the block. I call this the *vanishing piece effect*. Pieces that match the background tend to disappear, resulting in a hole in the block or making the block look transparent.

To work with contrast, sort your fabrics by light, medium, and dark. Determining the value of the fabric can be difficult. Contrast is affected by both the scale/print and the color of the fabric. A helpful way to determine contrast is to use a black and white copier. Cut small squares of fabric and copy them. Reducing the fabric to black and white gives you a way to see your fabric without being influenced by its color.

The second component is scale. Scale refers to the size and style of the print. Styles of fabric can include geometrics, florals, or abstracts. The size of

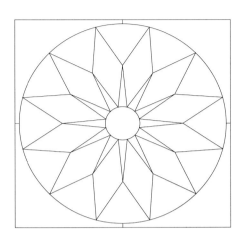

Fig. 3-7.

Fig. 3-8.

Fig. 3-9.

Fig. 3-10.

Plate 3-1. Use these types of prints with caution.

Plate 3-2. Appropriate fabric choices.

Fig. 3-11. Vary the scale of print fabrics adjacent to each other in your design.

each of these print styles can range from miniscule to gigantic. Scale is an important consideration when choosing fabrics for these patterns. *(Fig. 3-11)* As a general rule, solids accentuate, prints conceal.

There are a number of prints you should use with caution for these patterns. Do not use small multicolored prints or prints with high contrast. *(Plate 3-1)* Too many tiny bits of color tend to be confusing. High contrast prints like red and black or white and black can be too bold. They can overpower other fabrics and the design. Tiny prints with a monochromatic or muted color range are always safe choices. *(Plate 3-2)* You might want to choose small prints instead of solids. *(Fig. 3-12)* From a distance the print will read as a plain color, yet close up the small print will blend the seams, conceal tiny errors, and add interest.

Stay away from fabric without a definite color scheme. Some prints have no basic color. When you see a piece of fabric it should read a single color. There are fabrics that have equal amounts of more than one color. If pink and blue appear in equal amounts, is the fabric pink or is it blue? The print may appear muddy or prove distracting in the finished quilt.

Don't pick prints with blocks of color or tiny prints on open backgrounds. The pattern pieces may fall on different colored sections in the print or completely miss the motifs. From the same strip of fabric some pieces may be pastel blue while others are hot pink. Remember the pieces are small, and large prints may lose their charm when reduced to small fragments. *(Fig 3-13a)*

Be on the watch for prints that have a large amount of the same color as the block background. The vanishing piece effect can happen with sections of prints as well as with entire pieces. The effect may be breathtaking, almost like lace, or it may look as if the block had been randomly slashed. *(Fig 3-13b)*

The last factor in fabric selection is color. Choosing the colors for a quilt is a highly personal decision. I always encourage quilters to follow their own inner voices. There are basic rules and color schemes based on the color wheel, but so many times I have seen a quilter practically frozen by indecision, worrying about whether she has broken one of the "color rules." Over-analyzing the relationship between colors can make fabric selection agonizing. The rules and guidelines for color selection are to help us make choices and encourage us to expand our color use, not to constrain our natural color sense. There are a number of excellent books on color use for quiltmakers. For more information on color, scale, and contrast, see the books listed in the bibliography.

FABRIC PREPARATION

Pre-wash all fabrics and check fading and bleeding. It is always a good idea to sew together small samples of your fabrics before washing, to insure a dark color doesn't bleed into a light color. It is especially important if you are planning on air-drying your finished quilt. The thread in a seam can act as a wick and carry the darker color into the lighter as the quilt dries.

I strongly recommend heavy starching of all fabrics before cutting any pieces. I am frequently asked about my exact piecing. The secret of my great points, true circles, and flat blocks is starch. The more complex the piecing

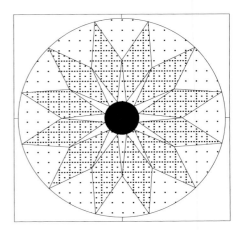

Fig. 3-12.

Fig. 3-13a.

Fig. 3-13b.

the more heavily I starch the fabric. Working with starched fabric is a revelation. The fabric cuts more accurately, marks more easily, and is fantastic to sew! The machine will never eat tiny points, and the fabric can't creep under the presser foot. I am convinced that simply starching the fabric can double your piecing skills. On average, the fabrics I used for the sample blocks were starched to about the stiffness of typing paper.The single drawback to starched fabric is in hand quilting. The starch will make the needle bind, and makes the seams harder to stitch. I always use starch on my fabrics, but use it sparingly when I plan to hand quilt. There are three ways to starch fabric:

SPRAY STARCH. I use this method for small pieces. The fabric is starched after it has been pre-washed and dried. In aerosol cans use professional or heavy starch. Original finish or spray sizing do not add enough body. To use a non-aerosol spray, mix liquid or powdered starch according to the package directions for medium to heavy starch. Use a plant mister or other pump style sprayer. To starch fabric with spray starch, place the fabric wrong side up on the ironing board and mist the fabric until it is slightly damp. Do not over saturate the fabric. Press, using a hot, metal plate iron until completely dry. Repeat the process three or four times to achieve the desired body. Starch's reputation for scorching and burning is undeserved. Light coats of starch with a hot iron will prevent sticking, scorching, or burning. If you do need to clean the iron, use terry cloth and hot water. In all but the worst cases, starch build up can be dissolved with plain hot water and slight abrasion from the terry cloth.

LIQUID STARCH. The fabric is starched after it has been washed, but before it is dried. Mix liquid or powdered starch according to the package directions for medium to heavy starch. Place the solution in a large container, like a wash basin or large kettle, so the extra solution can be poured into a sealed container to be reused. Place the damp fabric in the solution and thoroughly saturate the fabric. I suggest wearing rubber gloves to protect your hands. Starch isn't irritating to skin, just messy. Wring out the excess starch and line dry indoors or outside on a still day. Iron out the wrinkles while the fabric is still damp or mist the fabric with water as you press.

PROFESSIONAL STARCHING. This is my favorite method for large amounts of fabrics. Every quilter has faced the twisted yardages that come out of the washer. I've solved that problem. I send my fabrics to the laundry. Just think, no more washing and pressing yards of fabric rope! The laundry does all the work. The fabrics are washed, starched, and pressed. You may have to do some looking to find a laundry that cares for your fabrics as you do, but it is well worth it.

BASIC SUPPLIES

A SEWING MACHINE in good working order. The basic requirement is a dependable straight stitch. Features including needle down, electronic speed control/or slow speed, and a knee operated presser foot lift are advantageous. Use a new needle, size 11/70 or 12/80 and a fine thread in a neutral color. The success of the technique depends on the correct presser foot. I recommend three types of feet.

A straight stitch foot, or true ¼" foot is a necessity. (Fig. 3-14) Do not assume that the edge of the regular presser foot is a true ¼".

An open toe embroidery foot or no bridge embroidery foot. (Fig. 3-15) This foot is available as a generic foot for all machines. It was designed for embroidery or appliqué and gives unobstructed access to the needle and stitches.

A binder foot is my personal favorite. This foot was designed in conjunction with the bias binder for the home machine. It is a unique foot; the right hand toe and bridge of the foot have been literally cut away. (Fig. 3-16) This foot gives the feel and fabric manipulation of hand sewing on the machine. Like the open toe embroidery foot, it offers a clear view of the needle and stitches and simplifies complex matches. This foot is available as an optional foot for some brands of machines. The foot can also be made from a generic zigzag foot. To make a binder foot, cut or grind off the right toe and the entire bridge of the foot. Sand or file any rough edges and shape blunt cuts into gentle curves to allow the fabric to feed smoothly. Although my favorite, this foot can cause skipped stitches. The reduced surface area of the foot allows the fabric to move up and down with the needle, an effect called *flagging*. Flagging is most pronounced on soft fabrics. A heavy coat of starch will correct this problem.

CUTTING EQUIPMENT. Basic supplies include: a rotary cutter, an 18" x 24" rotary mat, and a 6" x 24" rotary ruler. The best rulers will be marked in a clear grid with both inches and ⅛ inches. You will also need sharp and comfortable scissors. I recommend spring action scissors to reduce hand fatigue and speed the cutting process. (Plate 3-3)

TEMPLATE SUPPLIES. Striplate piecing requires accurately made templates.

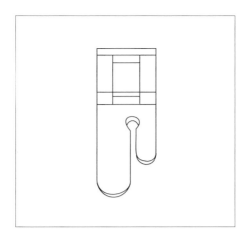

Fig. 3-14. Straight stitch foot.

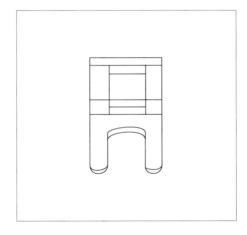

Fig. 3-15. Open-toe or no-bridge foot.

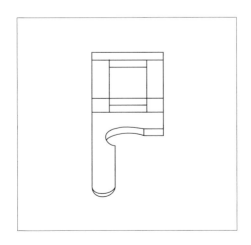

Fig. 3-16. Binder foot.

You will need clear template plastic (not gridded) to make the striplate template. A fine line permanent marker should be used to trace and mark the plastic. Transparent tape is used to protect pertinent markings from abrasion. A ¹⁄₁₆" punch is used for marking the matching dots. (See the resource list for companies that handle this special quilting punch.)

FABRIC MARKERS. Use markers that are fine line and very accurate. They should be easy to see and not brush away or disappear from the fabric. The marker should also write easily on the fabric, without you having to press down too hard or scribble back and forth to get a clear line. The marker should also be easy to remove. Last, the marker point must fit the ¹⁄₁₆" hole to mark the matching dots. I use a wide selection of markers, including #2B and #3B 0.5 mm mechanical lead pencil, quilter's silver pencil, water soluble graphite pencil, fine line chalk pencils, and white and colored pencils. *(Plate 3-4)*

ASSORTED SUPPLIES

PINS. Use long, thin, plastic or glass head quilter's pins. Throw away any pin that is dull, bent, or damaged.

IRON. Choose an iron that is hot on the cotton setting. It should be medium weight and well balanced. Steam is optional.

IRONING BOARD AND PRESSING PAD. Use a cotton ironing board cover and wash it frequently to remove the starch and keep the cover clean. A large light colored terry towel and 36" square of prewashed muslin will make an excellent pressing pad for the final pressing and blocking. Keep an extra can of spray starch and a plant mister of water at your ironing board.

Plate 3-3. Cutting equipment.

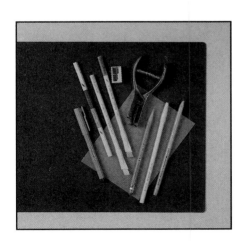

Plate 3-4. Fabric markers.

Basic Construction

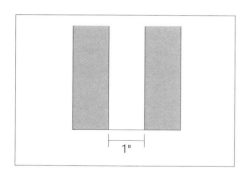

Fig. 4-1.

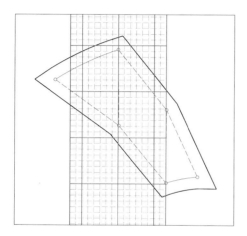

Fig. 4-2.

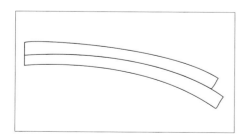

Fig. 4-3. Curved strips from mis-sewing.

The specific instructions and templates for the more than 20 blocks given in the pattern section, cover a wide range of sizes and skill levels. The patterns are given by style and in order of difficulty. The last chapter presents a few of the possible variations you can develop from these basic patterns. Before you begin working with the blocks, read the basic construction information in this chapter.

CONSTRUCTING AND USING THE STRIP STRATA

Before you can use the striplate template you will need to make strip pieced strata. The strata is a piece made of strips of fabric much like stripes on the flag. Each pattern will give specific directions for the width and sequence needed for that block.

ROTARY CUTTING. For striplate piecing the rotary cut strip matches a template. A strip wider than 1½" doesn't require special attention. Strips under 1½" can be considered miniature piecing and require careful cutting. The narrower the strip the more crucial that the cut be precise. Surprisingly, many of the errors in rotary cutting are because of the difference in rulers and patterns. Did you know that 1" may not be the same size

on all rulers? Most rulers and patterns are made as accurately as possible, but the width of the printed line and the thickness of the ruler can slightly distort the measure. I recommend you use the same ruler edge throughout the measuring and cutting process. Also check the ruler against the pattern. (Fig. 4-1) As an example, measure the striplate pattern piece for the 12" Whig's Defeat. This is a three strip piece, the diamond uses a 1½" strip that finishes 1" wide. Place your ruler over the diamond and measure from edge to edge. Do the lines on the pattern fall directly under the 1" mark? Let's say the pattern lines fall just inside the 1" mark. Cut the 1½" strip just inside the 1½" mark to compensate for the slight differences.

TIPS FOR ACCURATE ROTARY CUTTING.
- Always push the blade away from yourself as you cut.
- Hold the cutter at a slight angle to keep the blade in contact with the ruler edge.
- When cutting fractions of an inch, it is easy to misread and miscut. I use masking tape as a guide on the right side of the ruler, or I draw an X through the correct line on the ruler with a Vis-a-Vis® overhead projector pen. The pen makes a bold line on plastic and is easy to remove with

cool water and a soft cloth.

TRUE ¼" SEAM ALLOWANCE. An exact ¼" seam is required for stitching the rotary cut strips. To check the accuracy of your ¼" seam, do a stitching test. Using scrap fabrics, starch the fabric and cut three 6" x 1½" strips. Stitch the three strips together with a ¼" seam allowance. Press open the seams. Measure the middle strip. From seam to seam it should measure 1". *(Fig. 4-2)* If it doesn't measure 1", repeat the test, adjusting the way you feed the fabric under the foot.

STITCH LENGTH. Use a slightly shorter than average stitch for stitching together the strips. In regular strip piecing all the seams are straight and there is no strain on the seams. Striplates are angled pieces that form gentle inset piecing. Stitching the slight angle puts strain on the seams. A short stitch length prevents the seams from pulling open at the points and matches.

TIPS FOR SEWING STRAIGHT SEAMS. Do not pull on the top or bottom strip while sewing. It is so tempting to tug on the top strip to help align the edges. Tugging will stretch one strip while easing the other. The result is curved and uneven strips. *(Fig. 4-3)* The best way to insure straight seams is to pin the strips or treat both strips uniformly.

Another cause of curved strips can be the pressure on the presser foot. Many machines have adjustable pressure on the foot. When the pressure is too heavy the two strips will not feed evenly. Most frequently the top strip will appear longer than the bottom strip at the end of a seam. Check the machine instruction book to determine whether an adjustment is required on your machine.

CUTTING BASIC STRAIGHT STRIPS. This is simple beginner rotary cutting. Begin by folding the fabric in half, lining up the selvages. Minor deviations in grain line are unimportant. If the grain line is extremely bowed or skewed, the fabric should be pulled to straighten the warp and weft threads. Fold the fabric in half a second time, lining up the selvage edges with the first fold. *(Fig. 4-4)*

The first cut straightens the edges and is perpendicular to the folded edges. *(Figs. 4-5 and 4-6)* To cut the strips, place the ruler on the fabric at the correct width. Line up the cut edges with the vertical lines of the ruler and the folds with the horizontal lines. *(Fig. 4-7)* The strips are then stitched together with a ¼" seam allowance. Press open all seam allowances.

I use straight strips for almost all my quilts. Straight strips are a lazy, no-waste method of strip piecing. The one problem is the grain lines. Straight strips don't result in grain perfect pieces. Being realistic, they are not even close to correct! I don't usually care if the grain lines are off. Skewed grain lines don't affect the piecing process or the longevity of the quilt. In most cases the incorrect grain lines are indistinguishable on the finished quilt. I know that not every quilter is as easygoing about grain lines as I am. Many quilters find skewed grain lines unacceptable. Even I have to admit that there are times that true grain lines are required. One may be when working with stripes, plaids, or one-way designs. Another is when making an heirloom or contest quilt. Although it requires more time, cutting grain perfect strips is not difficult and the results are fantastic.

CUTTING GRAIN PERFECT STRIPS. Generally, the grain lines in a circle design all radiate from the center. *(Fig. 4-8, page 22)* Think of your pattern as a wagon wheel with the grain lines being the

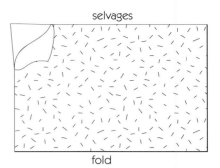

Fig. 4-4.

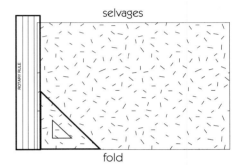

Fig. 4-5.

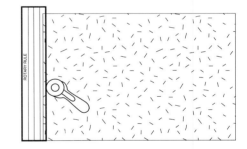

Fig. 4-6.

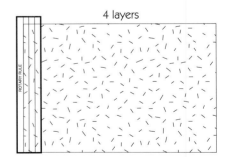

Fig. 4-7.

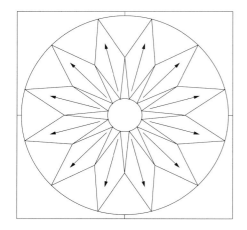

Fig. 4-8. Grainlines radiate from center.

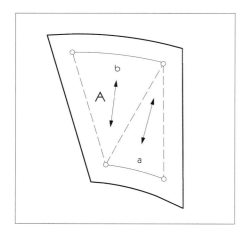

Fig. 4-9.

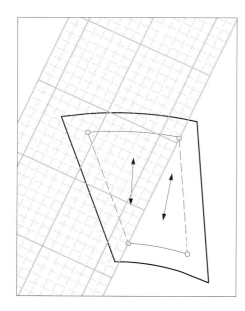

Fig. 4-10.

spokes. The patterns in this book indicate the correct grain. I will use the striplate pattern piece from Pickle Dish as an example for cutting grain perfect strips. Every striplate template is labeled with two sets of letters. *(Fig. 4-9)* A capital letter indicates the template and its location in the block. Lower case letters indicate the strips used to make the striplate. A two color striplate would be labeled side a and side b in addition to its capital letter.

To cut the strips for side b.

- Place your 6" x 24" ruler over side b. Line up the long edge of the ruler with the dotted line representing the strip pieced seam line. Look carefully at the illustration. *(Fig. 4-10)* The ruler is covering side b. The right-hand long edge of the ruler is on the dotted line.

- Transfer the straight of grain arrow from the pattern to the gridded ruler. *(Fig. 4-11)* A 6" piece of tape is adhered to the ruler parallel to the grain arrow.

- Cut an 18" x 45" piece of the required fabric. (I use a full width of fabric for the illustrations, but not every quilt requires this much fabric. The fabric requirements are determined by the size of the finished project. You could use a 22" or 18" square of fabric.) Open it to a single layer with the wrong side up. Have the selvages to the right and left with the raw edges on the top and bottom.

- Take the ruler off the pattern and place it on the fabric. Line up the tape/straight of grain parallel to the right selvage. The right edge of the ruler should go through the upper right-hand corner. Notice the ruler is at an angle across the fabric. *(Fig. 4-12)* This step is as simple as it seems. Pick up the ruler and move it to the

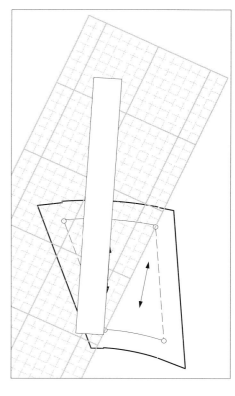

Fig. 4-11. Tape marking grain on ruler.

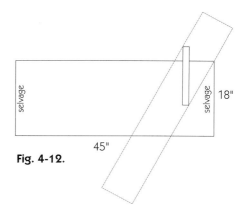

Fig. 4-12.

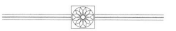

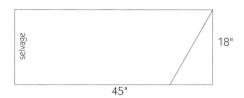

Fig. 4-13.

Fig. 4-14.

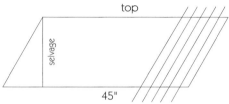

Fig. 4-15.

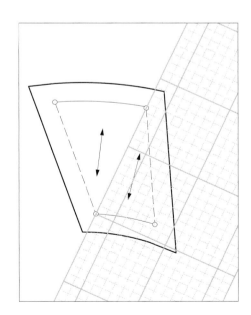

Fig. 4-16.

fabric. The ruler isn't turned or flipped or reversed. You're simply transferring the angle of side b to the fabric.

- Cut along the diagonal line formed by the edge of the ruler. (Fig. 4-13) That is the first cut of the strip. Sew the triangle made by the first cut to the other edge of the 18" rectangle. (Fig. 4-14) Think of this step as sewing selvage to selvage. Of course, the actual selvage should be cut off. The two pieces will form a diamond. All the strips for side b are cut parallel to this first cut. (Fig. 4-15) Don't worry about the seams. As each piece is cut, stack the strips. Do not turn or mix the strips, just stack them as they were cut.

To cut the strips for side a:

- Place your 6" x 24" ruler over side a. Line up the long edge of the ruler with the dotted line of the pattern piece. Look carefully at the illustration. (Fig. 4-16) The ruler is covering section a. The left-hand long edge of the ruler is on the dotted line.

- Transfer the straight of grain arrow from the pattern to the ruler with a piece of masking tape. (Fig. 4-17)

- Cut an 18" x 45" piece of the required fabric. Open it to a single layer with the wrong side up. Have the selvages to the right and left with the raw edges on the top and bottom.

- Move the ruler to the fabric. It is important that you understand this step. It isn't difficult, read carefully and follow along on the illustrations.

Notice how the ruler is placed on side a. The left edge of the ruler is on the dotted line and the tape is marking the grain line.

Pick up the ruler and move it to the fabric. (Fig. 4-18) Don't turn, twist, or reverse the ruler, just move it to the fabric. Line up the tape/straight of

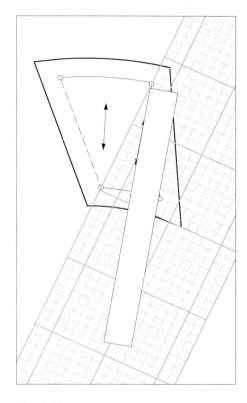

Fig. 4-17.

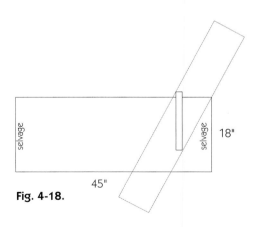

Fig. 4-18.

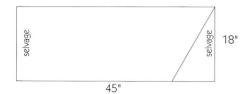

Fig. 4-19.

Fig. 4-20.

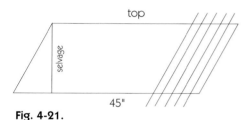

Fig. 4-21.

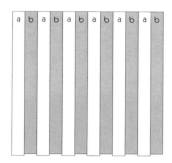

Fig. 4-22.

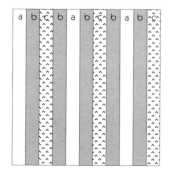

Fig. 4-23.

grain parallel to the right selvage. The right edge of the ruler should go through the upper right-hand corner. I *know* that the left edge of the ruler was lined up with the dotted line, but remember, the edges of the ruler are parallel. That means both edges are the correct grainline, and you can cut on *either* edge and have the correct cut. Notice the ruler is at an angle across the fabric.

- Cut along the diagonal line formed by the edge of the ruler. *(Fig. 4-19)* That is the first cut. Proceed as you did for the previous strips. *(Figs. 4-20 and 21)*

For the striplate patterns in this book, all of the strips must be cut slanting to the right on the wrong side of the fabric.

ARRANGING STRIPS FOR THE STRATA. For two-color striplates, arrange the strips in alternating colors. *(Fig. 4-22)* Begin with strip a on the left and end with strip b on the right. The sequence is a-b-a-b-a-b using all the strips. When cutting strips for two color striplates, cut an equal number of strips a and strips b. The pattern directions give the approximate number of striplate pieces you can cut along each 42" seam of the strata. An eight strip strata has seven seams. To determine the number of pieces this strata will yield, multiply the number of pieces per seam times seven.

For three-color striplates, begin with strip a on the left, then strip b and strip c. Every other strip will be a b strip, alternating with a and c. The sequence is a-b-c-b-a-b-c-b-a-b-c, *(Fig. 4-23)* use all the strips and always end with strip c. When cutting strips for three color striplates cut twice as many b strips as c or a. The pattern directions give the approximate number of

striplate pieces you can cut from every 42" strip b. In the sequence a-b-c-b-a-b-c-b-a-b-c there are five b strips. To determine the number of pieces this strata will yield, multiply the number of pieces per strip b times five.

STITCHING THE STRIP STRATA. Stitch the strips together with a ¼" seam allowance. Straight of grain strips will form a rectangle. Grain perfect strips will form an irregular diamond shape. To maintain the correct grain lines, all the top edges of the strips will form a reasonably straight edge, but the top edges won't be perfectly straight because the strips are cut with slightly different grainlines. The bottom edges may be very jagged because the differing grainlines result in varying length strips. Do not mix whole and pieced strips. Join the whole strips before adding the pieced strips. The seams in the pieced strips waste some fabric, grouping them together makes the best use of the fabric. After all the strips have been joined, press open all the seam allowances.

MAKING TEMPLATES

The template pattern has a number of key elements. *(Fig. 4-24)* The grain lines are marked on each section of the template along with the piece identification. The template shows the stitching line with a true ¼" seam allowance. The dotted line indicates the seam(s) of the strip piecing. Striplates are designed to facilitate piecing. Notice the seam allowance points are trimmed so the seams will line up perfectly without worrying about matching. The trimming of the points is a simple step that saves time and aggravation.

Making the template is an important step. A paper or plastic template needs

to be made for every piece in the pattern. Each template must be as accurate as possible. Paper templates are used for background pieces and center circles. Plastic templates are used for the striplate template.

To make a paper template, trace the template onto a plain piece of paper. Typing paper, freezer paper, or lightweight cardboard are suitable. Draw accurately and cut out the template. To use the template, pin the template to two to four layers of fabric, (Fig. 4-25) and carefully cut out the pieces. You can speed up the cutting process by rotary cutting the straight edges of large pieces. Place a ruler edge along the straight edges of the piece and cut with the rotary cutter. Hand cut any curved edges. This is an excellent method for the four corners on circle blocks.

To make the striplate template, carefully trace the piece on template plastic. Use a fine line permanent marker to mark all the seam lines, matching dots, and identification. Cover the markings with transparent tape to prevent the marks from wearing off. The striplate template is a one way pattern and cannot be reversed. To insure that the right side is always up, write the words *right side* on the correct side of the template. Cut out the template by carefully and precisely cutting on the ¼" line. This can be done with scissors or a rotary cutter and ruler. After cutting out the template, punch a ¹⁄₁₆" hole in the center of every circle.

Clipping the corners of the striplate template can make stitching the pieces easier. It is slightly less accurate than other matching methods but, what it lacks in accuracy is made up for by speed. By clipping the corners, you custom fit the templates to make

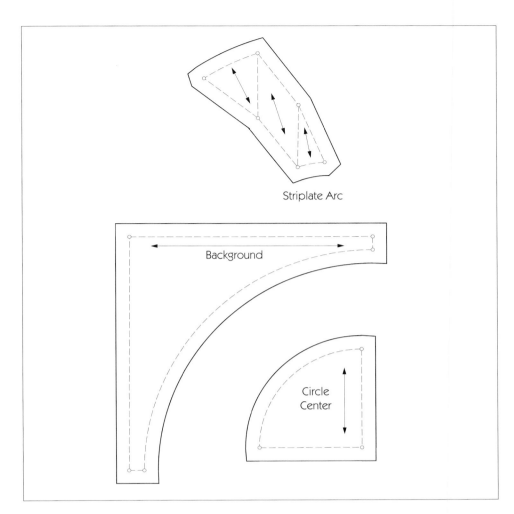

Fig. 4-24.

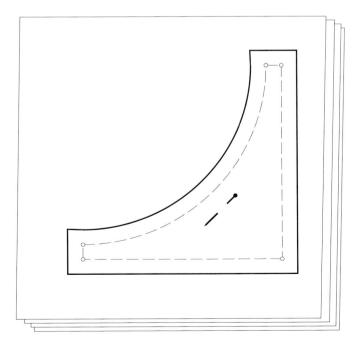

Fig. 4-25. Four layers of fabric.

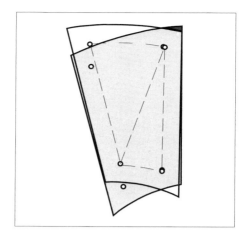

Fig. 4-26.

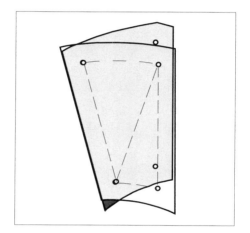

Fig. 4-27.

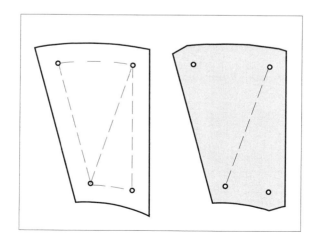

Fig. 4-28.

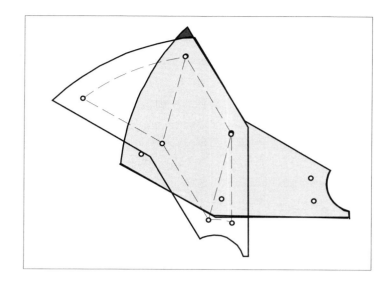

Fig. 4-29.

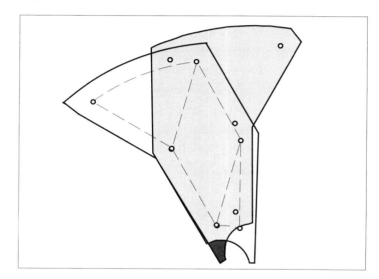

Fig. 4-30.

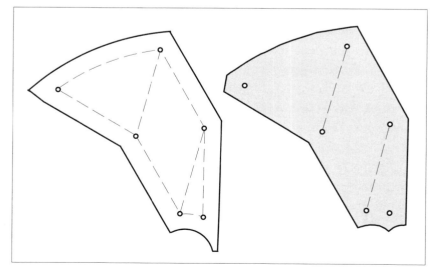

Fig. 4-31.

matching the seam allowances easier. To clip the corners will require lining up the template to the pattern just as they are sewn.

The simplest striplate to line up is the two-color striplate. Turn the plastic striplate template wrong side up. Line up the right edge of the template with the right edge of the pattern. Line up the matching dots. Notice there is a small triangle of template that extends beyond the upper right edge of the pattern. *(Fig. 4-26)* Do not worry about lining up any other point at this time; just look at the upper right edge and corner. That small triangle should be clipped away to make the edges match. Now slide the template to line up the left edge of the template with the left edge of the pattern. *(Fig. 4-27)* Line up the matching dots. Now the small triangle of template that extends beyond the pattern is in the lower left corner. Clip off this small triangle. Compare the clipped template to the pattern in the illustration. *(Fig. 4-28)*

Multi-pieced striplates are clipped the same way. Begin by making the basic striplate template and turn the template wrong side up. This next step will look odd. You are matching the first section of right edge of the template to the first section of the right edge of the pattern. *(Fig. 4-29)* Line up the matching dots. Notice there is a small triangle of template that extends beyond the upper right edge of the pattern. Do not worry about lining up any other point at this time, just look at the upper right edge and corner. That small triangle should be clipped away to make the edges match. Now turn and slide the template to line up the lower section of the left edge of the template with the lower section of the left edge of the pattern. *(Fig. 4-30)* Line up the matching

dots. A small section of template that extends beyond the pattern is in the lower left corner. Clip off this small triangle. Compare the clipped template to the pattern in the illustration. *(Fig. 4-31)*

TEMPLATES FOR PEOPLE WHO HATE TEMPLATES. No one enjoys tracing around templates. The process is acceptable on small projects, but it is overwhelming on large projects with hundreds or thousands of pieces. Striplate piecing does reduce the number of individual pieces, but it's still time consuming. There is a surprisingly simple solution – a rubber stamp of the template. Rubber stamps work excellently on two-color striplates. Imagine the joy and speed of stamping the pattern! Many quilters are familiar with the joys of stamping. Quilters frequently use rubber stamps to label their quilts. New manufacturing techniques have resulted in intricate, accurate stamps and water soluble inks. They are becoming so sophisticated they can realistically reproduce Victorian lithographs. Compared to lithographs, an accurate striplate template is a simple stamp to make. The phone book yellow pages can inform you of area office supply stores that offer custom stamp services. To have a template made you will need an accurate copy of the template pattern. A copy machine can distort the pattern, but it is acceptable if you double check the copy against the original to insure an accurate copy. Different copy machines have different amounts of distortion. If one copy machine doesn't make an accurate copy, try another, or choose photo grade for the copy selection. Photo grade copies take slightly longer to produce and tend to be more accurate. The pattern should look like the illustration: *(Fig. 4-32)* clean and clear, without any excess lines or dots on the

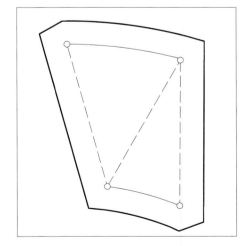

Fig. 4-32.

Plate 4-1.

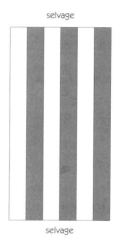

selvage

selvage

Fig. 4-33.

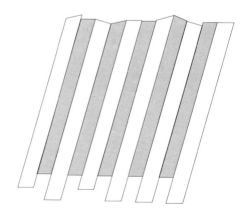

Fig. 4-34.

paper. Order a plain stamp – no handle and no pre-inking. A foam backing will help the stamp last longer and print more evenly.

After the rubber stamp is made, it will need to be mounted on a solid base. The base can be wood, plexiglass, or any solid material. To correctly place the stamp on the fabric, it is crucial to see the edges of the stamp. Opaque materials like wood should be cut to match the shape of the template. Transparent materials like plexiglass are cut in squares or rectangles.

To make a wood base. Use approximately a ¾" to 1" piece of solid wood. Glue the rubber stamp to the wood with a secure, long lasting glue that will not harm the rubber stamp (or foam). After the glue has dried, cut the wood to match the shape of the template. Trim the wooden base to match the stamp. Trim next to the cutting line on the stamp; this might include trimming away some of the excess rubber around the stamp. Glue a paper copy of the stamp to the base to help you place the template on the strip piecing. A handle may be added to complete the base. (Plate 4-1)

Plexiglass can also be used as a base. Cut the plexiglass in a square or rectangle the approximate size of the template. Trim away any extra rubber from around the stamp, trimming next to the cutting line. Glue the stamp to the plexiglass. Glue a paper copy of the stamp to the base to help place the template on the strip piecing. It acts as a guide for lining up the seams and pieces. Add the handle to finish.

These are only basic directions, you might choose to make the stamp base from a lovely hardwood and complete it with a beautiful finish and decorative handle. Or you might use styrofoam for

the base and adhere the stamp with double stick tape. To insure a long life for the stamp and the best results on your fabrics, use water soluble ink and ink pads available at craft stores. Experiment with ink colors for visibility and easy removal from fabrics.

MARKING AND CUTTING STRIPLATE PIECES

The templates will be drawn (or stamped) on the wrong side of the strata. Straight strip strata will form a rectangle. (Fig. 4-33) Grain perfect strata should slant towards the right. (Fig. 4-34) The reasonable straight edge of the grain perfect strata is the top edge. The templates are not reversible. The words RIGHT SIDE should be legible. To trace the templates on the fabric, line up the dotted line on the template with the seam line in the fabric strata. Make sure that section a is on strip color a. Start marking at one end of the first seam and mark pieces along the first seam. Skip any places a strip had to be pieced. Trace around the template carefully and mark all the matching dots. Place the pieces as close together as possible. After marking the first row, start at the bottom of the second seam. (Fig. 4-35) Turn the template one half rotation to place section a on strip a. Do not reverse the template, the words RIGHT SIDE should still be legible. The second row of pieces will interlock with the first row. Pieces may not share common cutting lines, so there will be a small amount of wasted fabric between the pieces. Mark the pieces as close together as possible.

Occasionally, when working with three or more colored striplates, the strip width may not perfectly match the template. Don't be discouraged, you won't have to rip! Small variations are a simple repair. Begin by tracing the upper half of the template onto the fabric. *(Fig. 4-36)* Mark the matching dots on that half, then carefully slide the template to line up the second half. *(Fig. 4-37)* Maintain the basic shape of the template. When these blocks are stitched, ease the longer pieces where necessary. After pressing, the small errors will not be noticeable.

TIPS FOR SCISSOR CUTTING PIECES. There is a maxim that says "Perfection is built on small details." That is especially true for piecing. Accurate cutting is essential to the perfect block. Most quilters use a rotary cutter, and as beginners received lessons on how to use the cutter, ruler, and mat. It is assumed as an adult we know how to use scissors in a way that's right. But our lessons happened when we were children. Our needs and expectations have changed, and there are refinements that will make cutting faster and easier. Many of these tips are basic and intuitive, but perhaps you might pick up an idea or two that will help you.

- To maintain accuracy, cut off most of the line made by the marker when traced around the template. The most important key is uniformity; if you cut off the line or choose to leave it on one piece, do all of the other pieces the same way.
- Handle small sections of fabric one at a time. Subdivide large groups of pieces into a manageable size. Thirty pieces drawn on a large piece of fabric should be rough cut to sections of three to five pieces before beginning the actual cutting.
- Work with the design of the scissors. If you are right-handed, hold the point away from you at a slight angle to the left. The piece you're cutting should

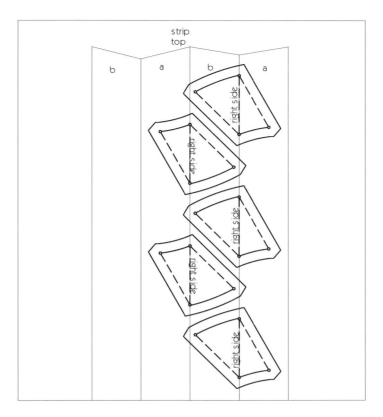

Fig. 4-35.

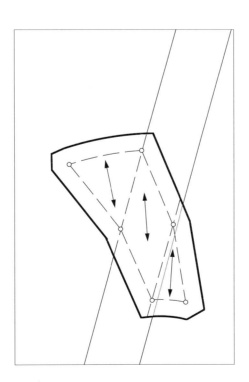

Fig. 4-36. Strip is too wide for striplate.

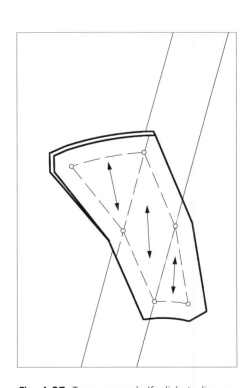

Fig. 4-37. Trace upper half, slide to line up second seam.

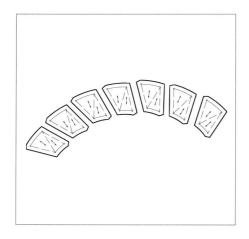

Plate 4-2.

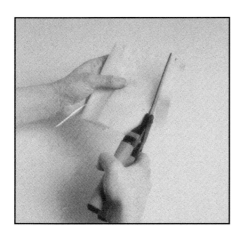

Fig. 4-38.

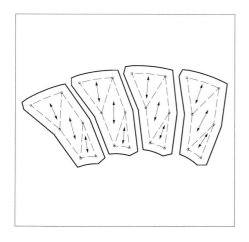

Fig. 4-39.

be held in your left hand, the scrap should fall away on the right side of the scissors. If you are left-handed, working with left-handed shears, hold the point away from you at a slight angle to the right. The piece you're cutting should be held in your right hand, the scrap will fall away on the left side of the scissors. A scissor cut is the most accurate when the piece you are cutting is resting on the lower blade. There are right- and left-handed shears and scissors. The difference is in the blade arrangement as well as the handles. The upper blade is on the right in right-handed shears and on the left in left-handed shears.

•The real trick is when left-handed people use right-handed or ambidextrous scissors that have a right upper blade. I am not left-handed but ambidextrous and do many things equally well, left- and right-handed. From my experience, I suggest holding the scissors flat in front of you pointed to the right. This angle gives a clear view of the cutting edge. I hold the piece I'm cutting in my right hand with the scrap falling away to the right of the scissors. (Plate 4-2)

•Use the entire blade length. The mid-portion of the blade should get the most use, not the points. In the mid-section, cuts are cleaner and more accurate. It is a matter of physics; the closer you are to the handle, the better the control of the blade. Begin the cut by opening the blades as far as a comfortable grip will allow. Line up the piece to be cut. Cut as long a line as possible with a single stroke. Long single cuts make smooth straight edges.

•Intricate cutting is a two handed skill. The scissors/shears are held relatively motionless; to turn a corner or a curve, turn the fabric, not just the scissors.

•Cut small pieces in mid air. You may rest your arms, but not the scissors/shears. I hold my hands and arms much the same way I do for knitting or crocheting. It brings the work close to me, and is also more ergonomically correct. The scissors/shears rest on the table when I am cutting yardages, multiple pieces, or large single pieces.

STITCHING THE BLOCKS

Striplate piecing uses a stitching method like hand piecing. It focuses on maintaining accurate piecing, not the ¼" seam allowance. The dots at the corners of the pieces are the sewing guide. Line up the dots and pin them together, even if the edges of the pieces do not match up perfectly. Sew dot to dot, disregarding any minor inaccuracy in the ¼" seam allowances.

MATCHING THE STRIPLATES. By nature of the design, circle patterns require intermediate matches. There are not 90° angles with simple matches. On the positive side, there are no difficult inset pieces. All striplate matches use the same basic method.

Lay out the striplate pieces required to make the block. Lay the pieces right side up. This will give you a clear idea of how the pieces fit together. A common mistake is to turn some pieces the wrong way. Notice how the piece is slightly pie shaped with a larger convex edge and a narrower concave edge. Think of piecing as putting pie pieces into a pie pan. The larger convex edges are the outside, the narrower concave edges are in the center. (Fig. 4-38 and 4-39) The pieces are sewn from the outside toward the center.

Begin with the two color striplate. This is an extremely easy match. Simply line up the clipped corners on the pieces and stitch through the dots. *(Fig. 4-40)* Sew edge to edge as you would any simple seam. *(Fig. 4-41)*

Next are three-color striplates. Place two pieces right side together. Notice you will be sewing an angled seam so the pieces do not line up perfectly at this place in construction, the convex angle on the top, the concave curve on the bottom. Don't panic! The trick is to break the seam into sections. Each section of this curve is a straight edge, and straight edges are easy to sew.

Start by lining up the first section. You will work from the outer edge to the first match.

A stab pin secures the first match. The stab pin match is a common match used for patterns like Flying Geese or Le Moyne Star. The match uses two pins. Using the matching dots as a guide, push the pin straight through the pieces. Don't tip the pin. Use a second pin as security, to help hold the match in place. *(Fig. 4-42)* The security pin is only temporary and is removed as it approaches the needle. The key to the perfect match is to keep the stab pin in place until the match is secured by the needle. As you sew, tip the stab pin up, taking care not to scratch the bed of the machine. Stitch right up to the pin. The shaft of the needle should brush against the pin, before removing the pin from the fabric. Stop with the needle lowered in the fabric. It is crucial that the needle stays in the fabric and is piercing the matching dot. Accuracy at this spot insures the perfect match.

To line up the lower half of the angle piece, lift the presser foot. Bring the lower edges of the pieces together, lining up the clipped corners. Both pieces will shift slightly, so the first half of the seam won't be lying flat. That is correct. *(Fig. 4-43)* Lower the presser foot and continue sewing to the edge of the piece.

Four-or-more-color striplates use the same matching technique as three-colored striplates. There are just more matches per piece. Just think in terms of sections. Begin on the outer edge and line up the first section. Stab pin the first match. Sew from the edge to the match. Stop with the needle lowered in the matching dot. Lift the presser foot and line up the edges for the next section. Pin the second match with a stab pin. You will have to tip the pieces to see the dot on the wrong side of the lower piece. If you desire you can omit the security pin on this match. Sew from the first match to the second. Stop with the needle lowered in the second match. Continue sewing and matching the pieces to the end of the seam. Personally, I pin the matches as I sew. You might prefer to pin all the matches on each piece before you begin sewing. Either method will work; choose the technique that gives the best results for your sewing style.

PRESSING. Pressing is an absolute necessity. It removes seam wells and makes the block lie flat. As a general rule for striplate piecing, press all seams open. Open seams reduce the bulk at intricate matches. It is the key to accurate matching and flat, smooth blocks. Open seams are more time intensive than the traditional method of pressing to one side but the results make it worth the effort.

There are two ways to press: finger pressing and iron pressing. I finger

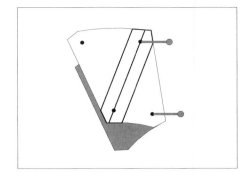

Fig. 4-40.

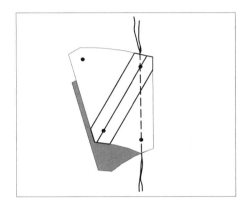

Fig. 4-41.

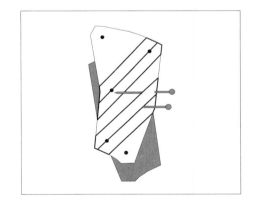

Fig. 4-42.

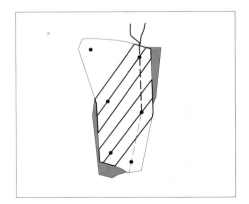

Fig. 4-43.

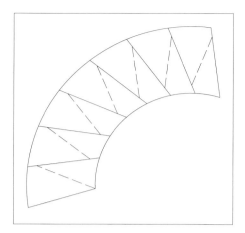

Fig. 4-44.

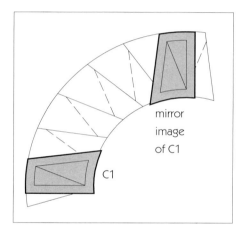

mirror
image
of C1

C1

Fig. 4-45. Trimming arc ends using arc end template.

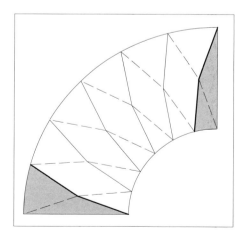

Fig. 4-46. Adding half pieces to complete arcs.

press all seams as I sew, even seams that will be iron pressed after the completion of the block. Finger pressing opens the seam allowances and makes ironing easier. It is an excellent method when sewing groups of pieces without crossed seams. To finger press, open the seam with your thumbs and index fingers. Then crease the seam with your thumb and index fingernails by pressing your fingers together and drawing them along the length of the seam.

COMPLETING THE ARCS. The partial circles or arcs, begin and end with half pieces. Partial circles are used in many patterns including Pickle Dish, Madras Interchange, Whig's Defeat, and Rattlesnake. The basic striplate pieces don't make an exact arc. The arc ends require half pieces.

Use Pickle Dish as an example for two-color striplates. When the seven striplate pieces are sewn together the arc is too long. Laid wrong side up, the left edge is too long on the outside curve, while the right edge is too long on the inside curve. *(Fig. 4-44)* This happens because the striplate pieces are cut as two full pieces. To make the arc fit the pattern, trim the ends of the arcs to form the required half pieces. In the pattern there is a pattern piece to use for trimming the arc ends, C1. Make a plastic template of this piece. The arc ends are mirror images. To make the correct cuts, use the template right side up for one end, and wrong side up for the other. *(Fig. 4-45)* Place the guide over the arc, lining up the seams with the lines of the template. Mark the correct arc ends and trim away the extra fabric.

Use a 9½" Whig's Defeat as an example for three-color striplates. Six full striplates are needed to make the six full diamonds required for each arc.

When the six striplates are sewn together the arc ends are irregular. Place the arc right side up to clearly see the piecing. Compare the arc ends to pattern piece C1. The right edge is too long on the outside curve and missing a piece on the inside curve. *(Fig. 4-46)* The left edge is too long on the inside edge, while missing a piece on the outside curve. You could sew an extra striplate piece to each end, but that wastes over half of each piece. A better method is to cut one striplate piece in half by dividing the diamond vertically. *(Fig. 4-47)* Use one half to fill in the left edge, the other half to fill the right edge. Sew the left side as usual from the outer edge toward the center. Sew the right edge from the center toward the outer edge. Make a plastic template of piece C1. The arc ends are mirror images, to make the correct cuts, use the template right side up for one end, and wrong side up for the other. Place the guide over the arc, lining up the seams with the lines of the template. Mark the correct arc ends and trim away the extra fabric. *(Fig. 4-48)*

COMPLETING THE BLOCKS. The striplate portion is the first section of the block to be sewed. The arc or circle needs a final press before setting it to the other pieces. Use a steam or dry iron. Press from the wrong side of the block. Do not slide the iron. Move in an up and down motion along the seam. Heavy steam or a light coat of spray starch will help to flatten even the most difficult seam allowance. Be extremely careful not to distort the block. Guard against any stretching of the arcs or circles when you press, if the arc is stretched it will not fit the rest of the block pieces. Use a blocking guide if you have any doubts about the exact size of the arc or circle.

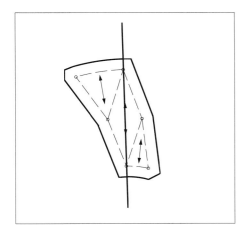

Fig. 4-47. Divide the diamond in half to complete the arc.

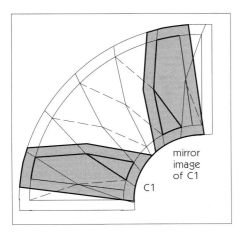

Fig. 4-48. Mark the correct arc ends.

mirror image of C1

C1

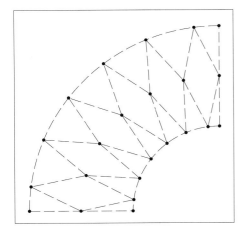

Fig. 4-49. Blocking guide made using matching dots on templates.

Blocking guides give an exact size of the finished arc or circle to help press the pieces to shape. *(Fig. 4-49)* To make your own guide use the plastic templates you made for the striplate and arc ends. Make a line drawing of the completed arc or circle on a plain piece of muslin. Remember to trace only the finished size of the pieces and omit the seam allowances. To trace the finished size, line the template up and mark the ⅟₁₆" holes used as matching dots.

Place the muslin on a firm padded surface like the ironing board. Place the pieced arc or circle right side down on top of the blocking guide. Pin the arc to the blocking guide. Stab the pins through the block into the padded surface. *(Fig. 4-50)* The pins will hold better if they are put in at an angle, leaning away from the piecing. *(Fig. 4-51)* Line up every piece with its corresponding section on the guide. Ease or stretch the block as necessary. Press the block to shape. Use heavy steam or mist the block with plain water. Gentle tugging or easing is allowed. After pressing, let the pieced block dry and cool before removing the pins.

SEWING THE CENTER CIRCLES. After the circle is blocked, set the center circle. I recommend hand appliqué for full circles or small partial circles. Hand appliqué guarantees a true circle without points. I use a beginner's method of appliqué, and have had excellent results. With this method even partial circles begin as a full circle. I prefer to start with a full circle for two reasons: it's easier to obtain smooth edges, and it allows for mistakes. It can be difficult to accurately fit a small quarter circle to the block. No matter how carefully it is appliquéd, the corner often becomes skewed. *(Fig. 4-52)* A full circle can be

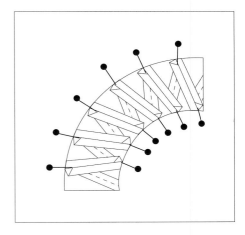

Fig. 4-50.

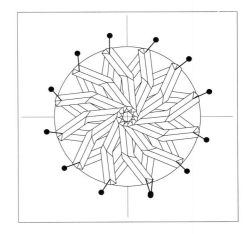

Fig. 4-51.

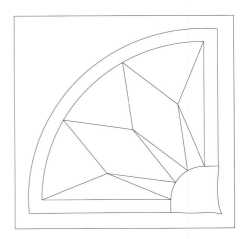

Fig. 4-52. Accurately fitting quarter circles to blocks is difficult; corners may become skewed.

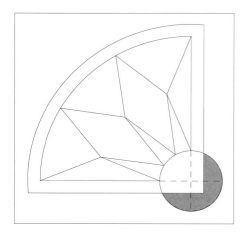

Fig. 4-53. Use full circle and trim to make true 90° corner.

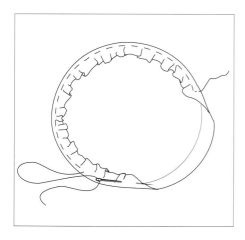

Fig. 4-54.

set in place and then the corner is trimmed. *(Fig. 4-53)* This method is part of the "sew first, cut second" rule of piecing. It's a foolproof method to get neat, true 90° corners.

To appliqué. Cut a cardboard template the finished size of the center circle. I use manila file folders or lightweight cardboard like shirt boxes. Cut the center from the fabric, allowing a ¼" seam allowance. Stitching in the seam allowance, hand stitch around the center with a running stitch. Use hand quilting thread and leave long thread tails. Center the cardboard template on the wrong side of the fabric. Pull on the thread tails to fit the fabric circle to the template. *(Fig. 4-54)* Tie the thread tails in a knot to hold the shape. Smooth out the easing, and press. Do not remove the cardboard. The cardboard form remains in the circle during appliqué to insure a perfect circle. Place the center in the correct location on the block. Working on the right side of the block, use a blind stitch to appliqué the circle. Take shallow stitches that do not catch the cardboard. When the appliqué is completed, press the entire block and let the block cool before removing the cardboard. To remove the cardboard, clip and remove the hand running stitch and remove the cardboard form through the opening in the back on the block.

SEWING THE BACKGROUND. Arcs and full circles can be machine pieced to the background. Sewing this curved seam is like handling any other curve. The smoothest curves result from sewing with the convex piece on the bottom and the concave piece on the top.

When stitching arcs, place a pin at the mid-point of the arc. Then place a pin at each end. On large arcs use extra

pins to hold the pieces in place. The bias edge of the concave piece will stretch to fit the lower curve. *(Fig. 4-55)* Sew slowly, using the point of a pin or seam ripper to help align the seam allowances.

When setting in a full circle, seam together the four corner pieces to make the background. Press open the seams. *(Fig. 4-56)* Visualize the circle as a clock face. Pin at 12, 3, 6, and 9, then pin at every point around the circle. Stretch the background curve as you pin. Sew with the circle on the bottom and the background on the top. *(Fig. 4-57)*

There is one small problem. When the pieces are sewn with the striplate piece on the bottom, the matching points on the striplate piece are not visible. If you've been accurate till now, the points won't be a problem. But, occasionally you may sew through the points on the arcs or miss them completely. Inaccuracies happen to the best quilters. When this happens there is no alternative to ripping. Since we can't guarantee all the points will always be perfect, we need to find an easy way to rip. Like every other part of sewing, ripping is a fine art. The easiest way to rip out stitches is to use a seam ripper to cut every fourth stitch on the bobbin side of the stitching. To remove the stitching simply pull on the top thread and the stitches will slide apart.

For the occasional mistake ripping is a good option, but there are times that it would be nice to try out a seam without having to worry about ripping. The solution is Wash Away Basting Thread®. This magic thread is made of a water soluble material. It looks like white thread, but it disappears when it is steam pressed. For tricky piecing, Wash Away Basting Thread® is a time saver. It can be used in the bobbin or

needle, but it is a very fine thread and is less apt to break in the bobbin. To use, stitch the curve as normal and check for any errors in stitching, steam press any incorrect portions of the seam and gently tug until the pieces pull apart. Line up the seam to correct the problem and restitch the curve with regular thread. Wash Away Basting Thread® is not permanent, so the entire seam must be restitched with regular thread. It does take extra time to stitch every curve twice but the alternative is time-consuming ripping, which can cause problems. Massive amounts of ripping stretch the block and can tear fabrics. Frequent stitching and knotting can literally wear out the seam line. Wash Away Basting Thread® is a great alternative.

Complete the background by pressing the seam. In most cases the seam should be pressed away from the striplate section. The seaming in the striplate section is heavy and the seam naturally wants to lie towards the background. There are a few exceptions to this rule — when the fabric is a very light colored fabric and the striplates are very dark colored, and on complex matches like Double Wedding Ring variations. Pressing the seams open can alleviate problems caused by shadowing of dark colors and can make narrow points easier to match and make them lie flat.

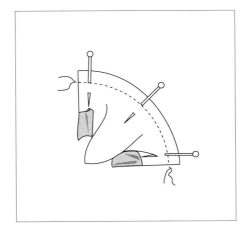

Fig. 4-55. Pinning and stitching a quarter arc.

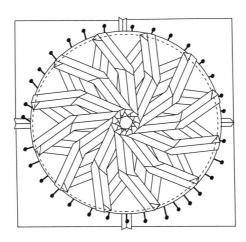

Fig. 4-56. Pinning background to circle.

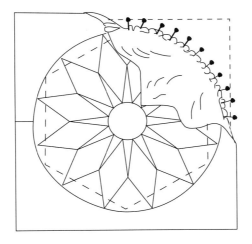

Fig. 4-57. Stitching background to circle.

Patterns

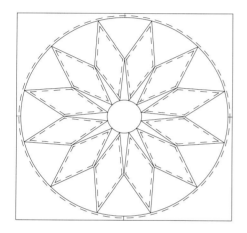

Fig. 5-1.

Fig. 5-2.

Choosing patterns for a book is the most difficult part of writing. There are thousands of patterns that could be included for use with this technique, but the choices have to be limited. I had to choose between offering a wide variety of block patterns, or giving detailed instructions for specific quilts. I compromised. The deciding factor was the patterns themselves. Striplate patterns can be difficult to draft, and I as a quilter would prefer the block patterns to quilt patterns. So in the end, I chose a wide variety of blocks, with directions.

There are 22 patterns, plus a dozen variations. The patterns range from simple to advanced. Many of the patterns were inspired by antique quilts. Some of the variations, including Candy Dish, are my own design. The patterns in this book are intended to appeal to the intermediate up to the advanced quiltmaker. Each pattern will list specific directions for that pattern. On some patterns there will be directions for variations or alternative sets. The directions do not explain basic piecing procedures. The bibliography lists books on beginning quiltmaking.

The patterns are presented by pattern type and in order of difficulty — two-color striplate, three-or-more-color striplate, and multi-ring designs.

The patterns were designed to be user friendly. The block sizes were determined by the strip widths used for the striplate templates. I designed the majority of the blocks with strips measured in inches or eighths of inches. Two advanced blocks require a strip cut to 1/16" of an inch. The patterns give detailed instructions to make this as simple as possible.

<u>YARDAGES AND PURCHASING FABRIC</u>

I suggest that you make a single block of the pattern before starting a larger project. Use the block to try out the fabric combinations and the sewing procedure. Purchase 1/3 yard of each fabric you want to include in your block. A third of a yard is enough for straight cut strips, with a little left for changes if you find the original color placement doesn't work. For large blocks, make sure you buy enough yardage for the block background. That is the largest piece in the block and can require 1/3 to 1/2 yard by itself. The trial block is the most important step in the design process. Many times fabrics that looked gorgeous in a stack look awful in a block. Trying out the fabrics insures you are buying yardages of the fabrics you really want and are going to use.

After you have constructed the sample block and made your final decisions, you will want to purchase the fabric for your project. The yardage is determined by the size of the project, the number of fabrics, and their placement. With so many variables it is impossible to give the yardages for every possible size and variation for each pattern in this book. There are math or geometry methods you can use to detemine the exact yardage that you need, but calculating this isn't an enjoyable process. Rather than doing math, I make a generous guess based on the yardages needed to complete my sample block. Occasionally I purchase fabric without a project in mind. In general, three yards of fabric is a safe amount to purchase for the pieced sections of the quilt. The larger background pieces require a five-yard minimum of fabric.

QUILTING. The tiny pieces and highly structured design of striplate patterns are well suited to outline quilting. I recommend ¼" or ⅛" outline quilting around alternating rows of pieces. *(Fig. 5-1)* Another choice is to have the quilting lines radiate from the center of the block. *(Figs. 5-2 and 5-3)*

The large open spaces of striplate patterns are the perfect place for intricate motif quilting. *(Fig. 5-4)* The backgrounds can be filled with feathers, floral motifs, and folk art patterns. Excellent sources for pattern ideas include appliqué patterns and quilting pattern books. The bibliography lists many of my favorite pattern sources.

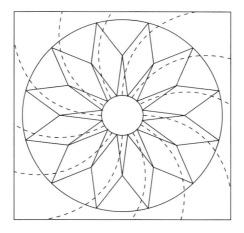

Fig. 5-3.

Fig. 5-4. Typical quilting motif.

Plate 5-1. Pickle Dish. 42" x 42".
Bright blue, white, and red with assorted other primary color prints,
cotton. Set with blue border and finished with multicolored prairie
points. Straight set variation with square in square corner block.
Machine quilted.

TWO-COLOR STRIPLATE PATTERNS

PICKLE DISH

This variation of the Double Wedding Ring pattern is sometimes called Indian Wedding Ring. The traditional arcs are divided into triangles rather than squares. Wedding Ring patterns can be set diagonally or straight. The sets appear only slightly different, but there is a large difference in how easy they are to machine piece. The determining factor for the set is the corner block.

Straight set, the easiest to sew, requires a pieced corner block. *(Fig. 5-5)* The corner block must be quartered like the four patch. With the divided corner block, the center sections can be divided into four pieces, making the ring a simple Four Patch block. The set is extremely easy to sew and the straight edges make the quilt easy to bind. The single disadvantage is the pieced center sections.

The diagonal set is visually more interesting than straight set. *(Fig. 5-6)* The uneven edges give the design an excitement that is lacking on the straight edge sets. The diagonal set can be used with any corner block, but, is required with a pieced or solid block that cannot be quartered, like Square In Square or LeMoyne Star. *(Fig. 5-6a)* Diagonal set uses a single piece center section and requires intermediate sewing skills to set and bind.

The two sets require vastly different directions. The first set of directions will be for making a single block of the straight set. The second will be for the diagonal set.

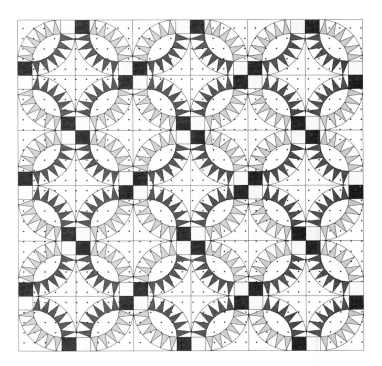

Fig. 5-5. Straight set.

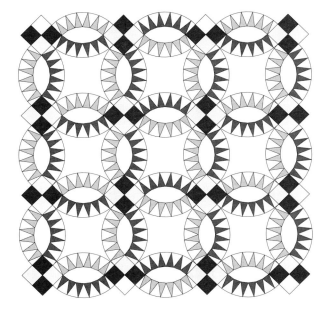

Fig. 5-6. Diagonal set.

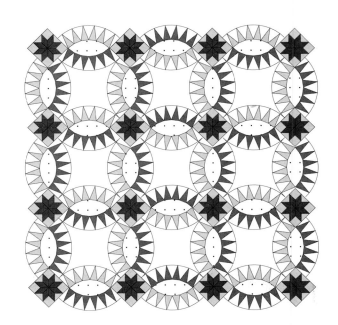

Fig. 5-6a. Diagonal set, with LeMoyne Star.

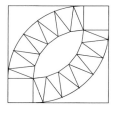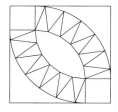
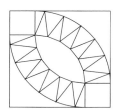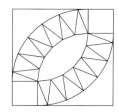

Fig. 5-7.

STRAIGHT SET

Block size: 12"

There are seven striplate pieces in each arc.

The strips are cut

2½" for side a

2¼" for side b

Approximately 17 striplates can be cut along each 45" seam.

The pattern offers three corner block versions, choose the Four Patch piece D. Cut four D for every corner block. For this set use the quarter version of piece A, the center section.

<u>Block Directions</u>

To make one unit. Four units are required for each block. *(Fig. 5-7)*

- Piece two arcs, joining 7 striplate pieces to make each arc. Use template C1 to cut the arc ends.
- For the Four Patch corner, stitch two piece D's to the ends of one arc. Press the seams towards the corner squares. *(Fig. 5-8)*
- Stitch the shorter arc to the ellipse B. Press the seam towards the ellipse.
- Stitch the longer arc to the other side of ellipse B. Press the seam towards the ellipse.
- Join one piece A to each side of the arcs to complete the unit. *(Fig. 5-9)* Press open the seams. Join four units to make one 12" block. *(Fig. 5-10)*

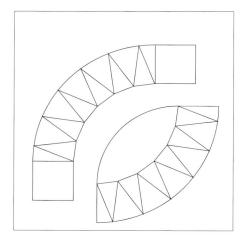

Fig. 5-8.

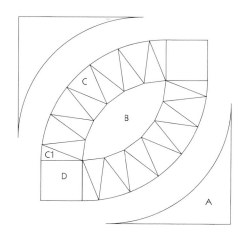

Fig. 5-9.

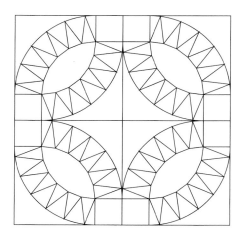

Fig. 5-10.

DIAGONAL SET

The diagonal set does not use a true block pattern. The quilt top is constructed from block sections rather than identical blocks. The illustration of the basic nine ring configuration highlights the four block sections. *(Fig. 5-11)*

The exterior arcs used to complete the edges are section 1. The total number of exterior arcs in a quilt depends on the rings in the quilt, but there are never fewer than four and they are always an even number. The arc sections are made of one arc and one elipse. *(Fig. 5-12)*

The left corner ring used to start the quilt, is section 2. The section is made of four arcs, four corners, and a center.

The edge ring is used on the left and upper edges of the quilt; it is section 3. The number of times this section is used depends on the rings in the quilt. It can be any number, even or odd. Notice the left edge rings are turned a different direction than the upper rings, but they are identical, four arcs, two corners, a center, and one ellipse. The basic ring is used in the quilt body and forms the right and lower edges and corner; it is section 4. The number of times this section appears in the quilt depends on the quilt size, but usually this ring is the most frequently used section. The section is made of four arcs, one corner, a center, and two ellipses.

Block size: approximately 8½"

To determine the width of a row of rings, multiply the number of blocks times 8½". Add to that total 4½" for the two exterior arcs. A nine ring configuration, 3 blocks by 3 blocks would measure about 30" square (compared to a nine block straight set measuring 36").

There are seven striplate pieces in each arc.

The strips are cut

2½" for side a

2¼" for side b

Approximately 17 striplates can be cut along each 45" seam.

The pattern offers three corner block versions, choose either:

Square in Square, pieces F and E. Cut four F and one E for every corner block.

LeMoyne Star pieces G and H. Cut eight of each piece for every corner block. See the construction notes for further information about piecing this block.

Use the entire piece A for the center section.

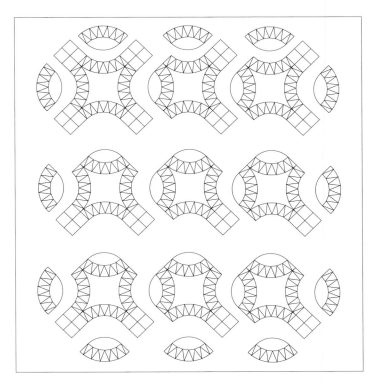

Fig. 5-11.

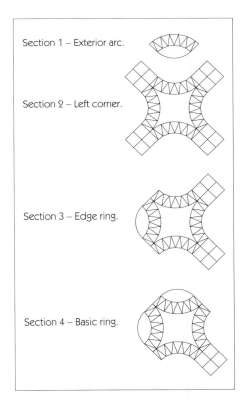

Section 1 – Exterior arc.

Section 2 – Left corner.

Section 3 – Edge ring.

Section 4 – Basic ring.

Fig. 5-12.

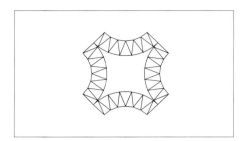

Fig. 5-13.

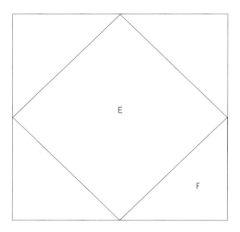

Fig. 5-14a. Square in Square.

Fig. 5-14b.

Block Directions

- Piece the arcs, joining 7 striplate pieces to make each arc. Use template C1 to cut the arc ends.
- Join four arcs to each center, this is the basis for all the ring sections. *(Fig. 5-13)* I suggest pressing open the seams that join the arcs to the center. The pressed open seams will make it easier to add the adjoining arcs, and the block will be smoother.
- Construct the corner blocks. For the Four Patch block stitch together four piece D's. For the Square in Square stitch a piece F to each side of square E. *(Fig. 5-14a)* For the LeMoyne star stitch together 8 piece G's to make the star. *(Fig. 5-14b)* Set in 8 square H's around the star. To make the block a 3" square trim off the points of every other square. This method precludes the use of small triangles and gives a truer 3" square.
- Join the corner squares to the correct locations on the ring sections. Press the seams towards the corner blocks.
- Complete the ring sections by adding the appropriate ellipses to each section.
- Join the ring sections block by block, beginning with the left corner block. Work to the right across the first row of rings. *(Fig. 5-15)*
- Begin the second row, joining the right edge ring to the left corner ring. *(Fig. 5-16)* Continue to add individual ring sections to the quilt body, working to the right across the second row. *(Fig. 5-17)*
- Continue adding individual ring sections by rows working left to right from the top to bottom. This method of joining individual sections to the quilt body is an easy way to join diagonal set Wedding Rings by machine. *(Fig. 5-18)*
- Finish the quilt top by adding the exterior arcs.

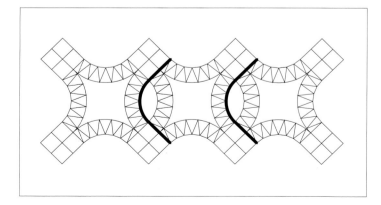

Fig. 5-15.

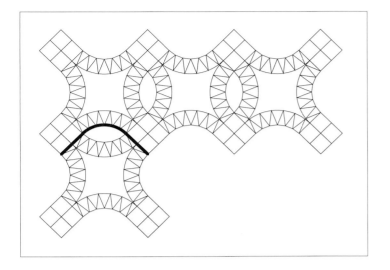

Fig. 5-16.

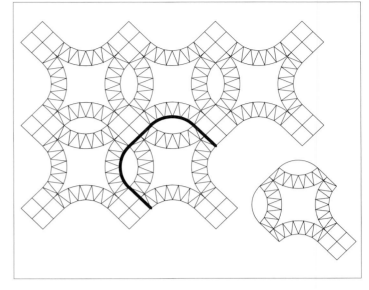

Fig. 5-17.

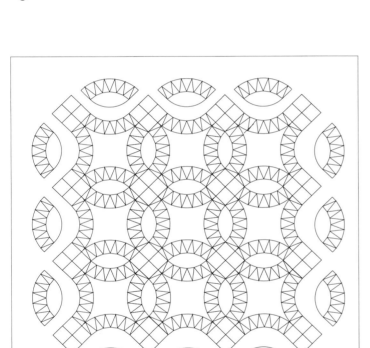

Fig. 5-18.

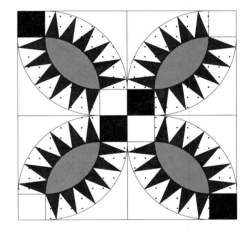

Pickle Dish.

Pickle Dish on point.

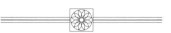

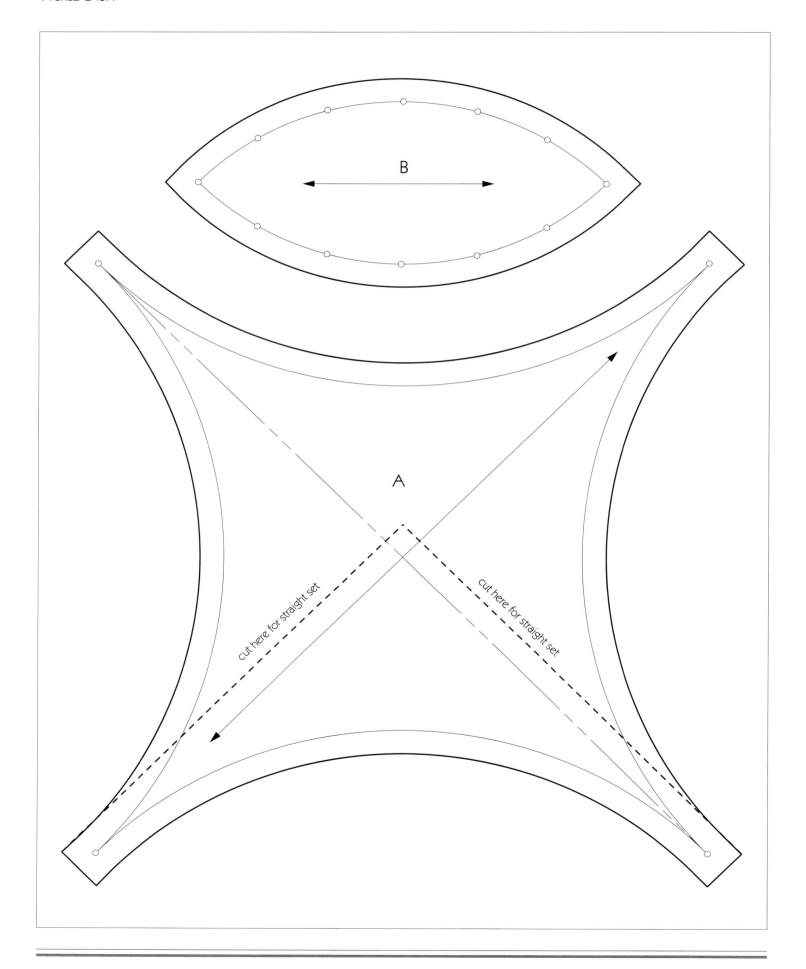

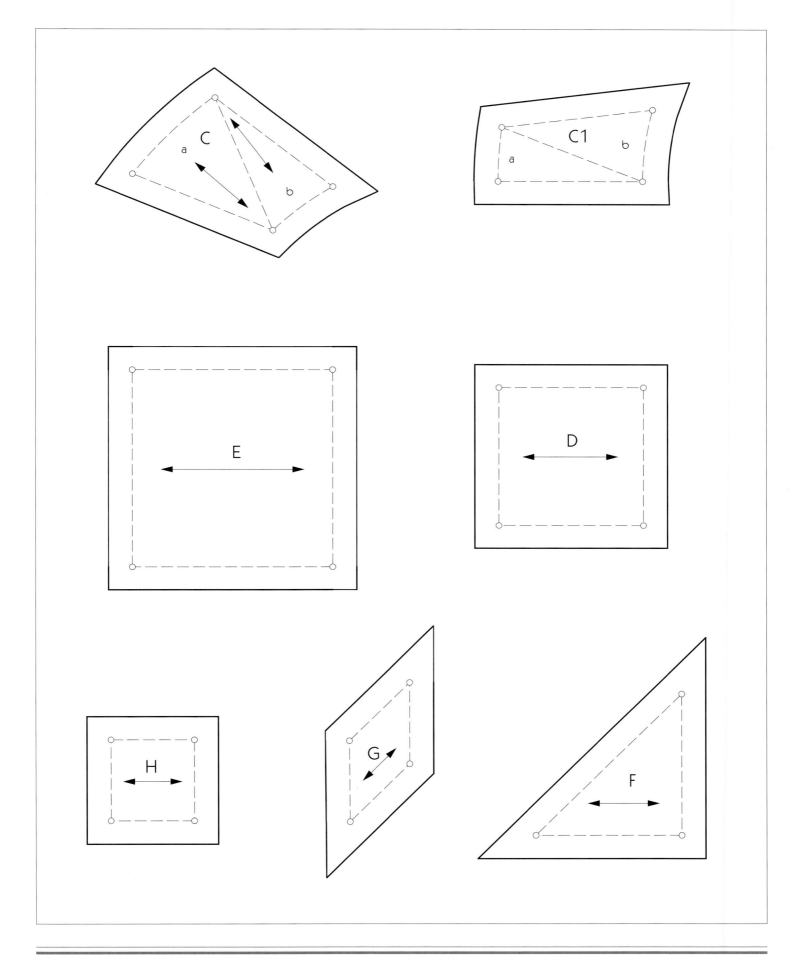

Plate 5-2. Circular Saw. 30" x 30".
White and hot pink prints, cotton. The four blocks are sashed and bordered to match the block interior. Unquilted.

CIRCULAR SAW

Block sizes: 7" and 12"

There are five striplates in each arc or 20 for each block.

The strips for the 7" block are cut

    2" for side a

    1¾" for side b

Approximately 21 striplates can be cut along each 45" seam.

The strips for the 12" block are cut

    2¾" for side a

    2" for side b

Approximately 13 striplates can be cut along each 45" seam.

Block Directions

- Piece the arcs, joining 5 striplate pieces to make each arc. Use template E1 to cut the arc ends. *(Fig. 5-19)*
- Join the arcs to the block center, A.
- Join piece B to complete the arcs.
- Stitch two arc sections to sashing C, to make the left half of the block. Repeat for the right half of the block. Press the seams toward the sashing.
- To make the vertical sashing strip, stitch sashing piece C to square D. Press the seams away from the square.
- Join the block halves to the vertical sashing to complete the block.

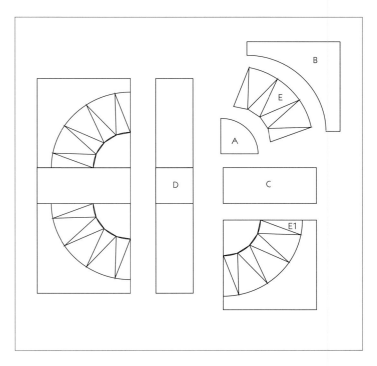

Fig. 5-19.

Circular Saw.

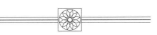

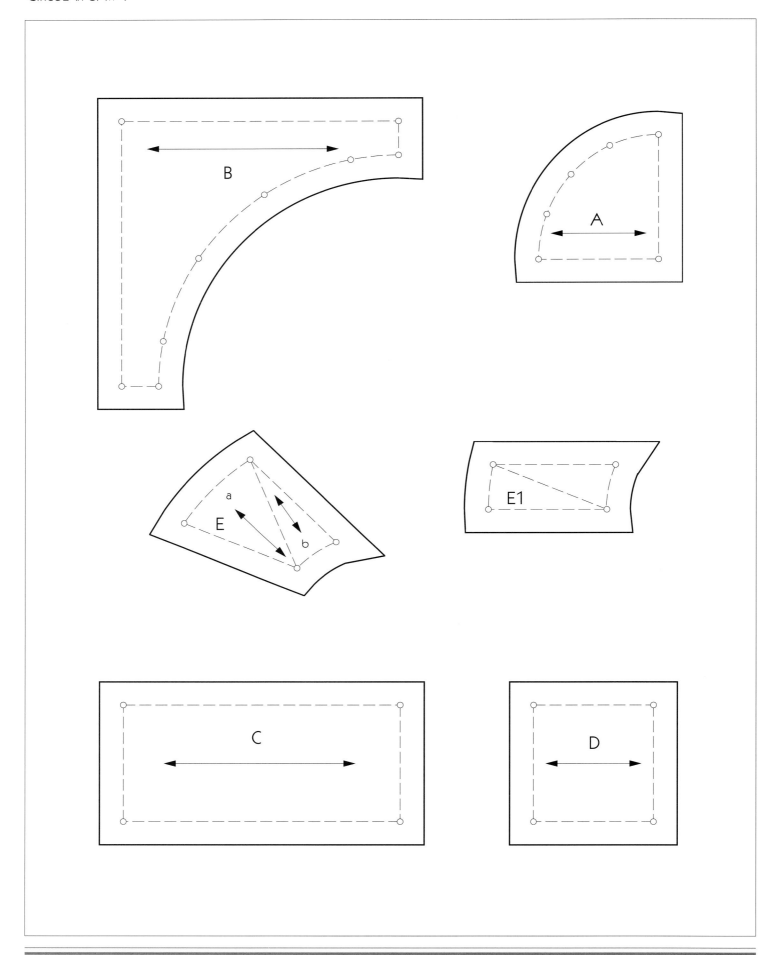

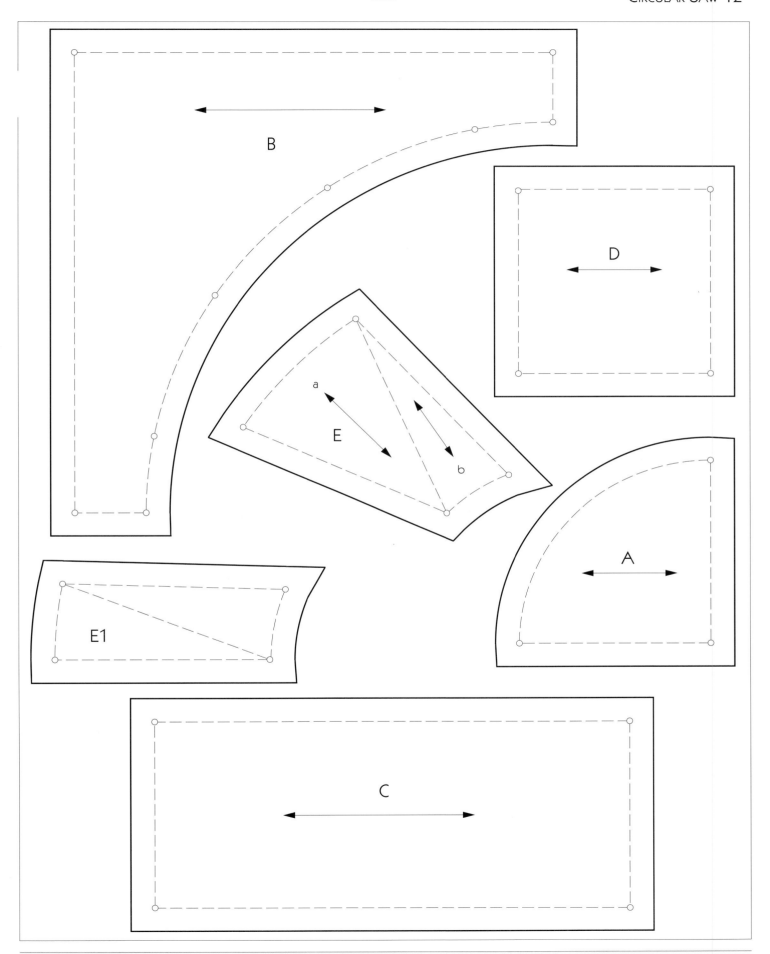

Plate 5-3. Friendship. 32" x 32".
Cream, brown, and red, with accents of navy and gold, cotton. Four
blocks sashed and bordered. Unquilted.

FRIENDSHIP

Block size: 12"

There are five striplate pieces in each arc or 20 in each block.
The strips are cut

    2½" for side a
    2¼" for side b

Approximately 14 striplates can be cut along each 45" seam.

Block Directions

- Piece the arcs. Unlike other striplate arcs, Friendship does not use half pieces on the arc ends. *(Fig. 5-20)* To piece the arcs, join four striplate pieces. For the final piece in each arc use the fifth striplate piece. Separate side a and b, by ripping the seam between the pieces. Discard side b. Press side a to remove the crease along the seam line and join it to the correct end of the arc.

- Join pieces A, B, and D to the striplate arc. Press the seams to one side, preferably away from the striplate arc. Make four sets of A, B, D, and the striplate arcs. *(Fig. 5-21)*

- Set in the block sides E. For accurate matches, mark and use the matching dots on all the block pieces.

- To complete the block, join the four quarters. Traditionally the four D pieces form the block center.

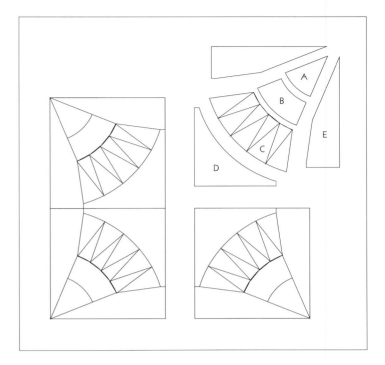

Fig. 5-21.

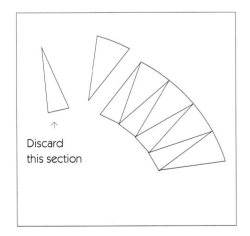

Fig. 5-20.

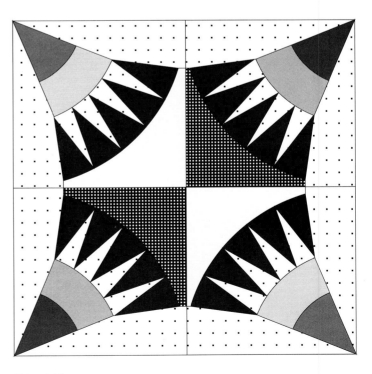

Friendship.

51

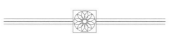

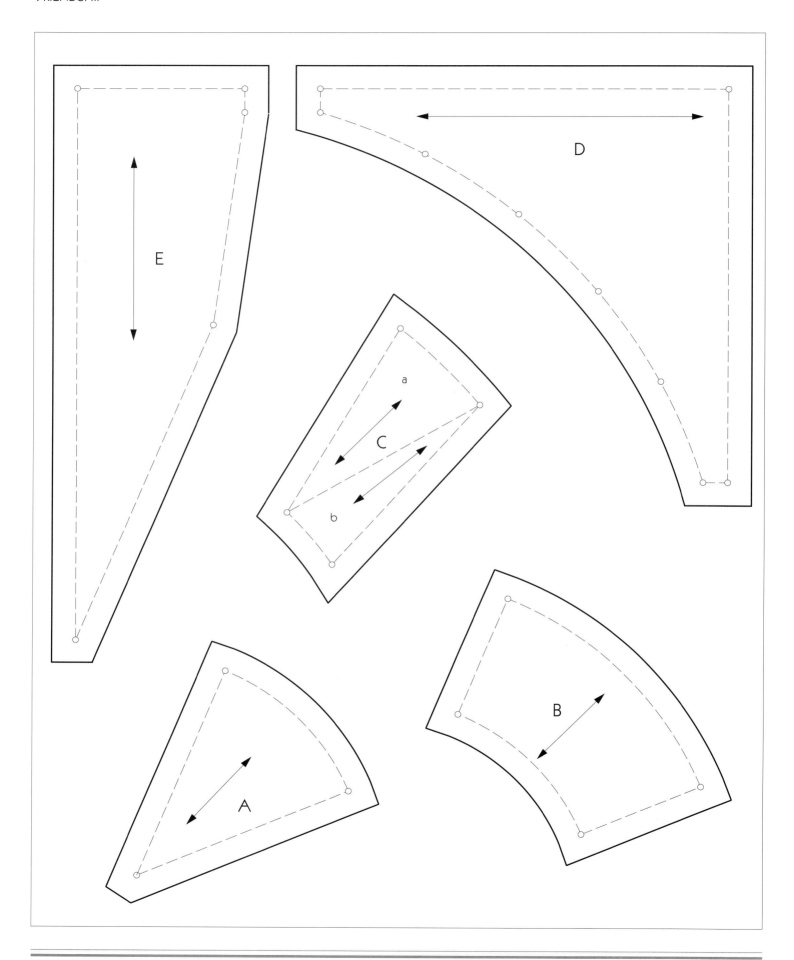

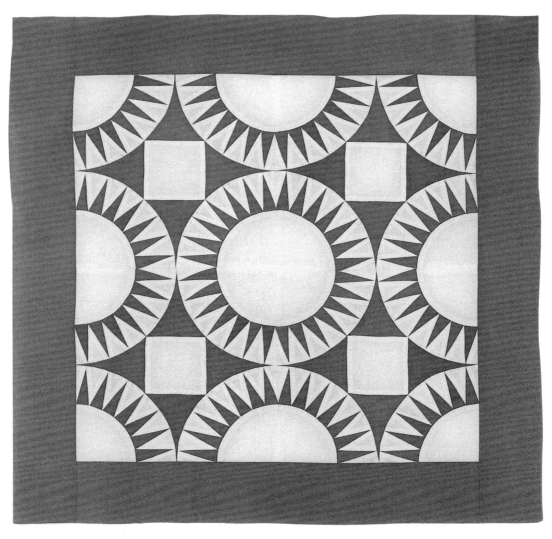

Plate 5-4. Whig's Defeat Sunburst. 26" x 26".
Kelly green and white cotton. Four blocks with green border.
Unquilted.

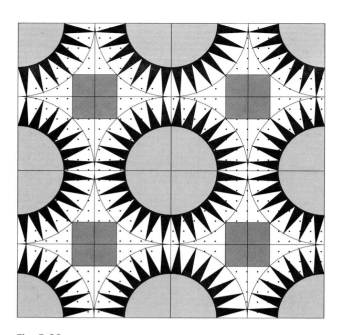

Fig. 5-22.

WHIG'S DEFEAT SUNBURST

Block size: 10"

There are 8 striplate pieces in each arc or 32 in each block.

The strips are cut

    2¼" for side a

    2" for side b

Approximately 15 striplates can be cut along each 45" seam.

<u>Block Directions</u>

- Piece the arcs, joining 8 striplate pieces to make each arc. Use template B1 to cut the arc ends.
- Join the arcs to the block corner A to make the corner unit. Press the seam toward the corner. *(Fig. 5-23)*
- Join four piece C's and one piece D to make the block center. Press the seams open.
- Stitch the corner units to the block center. Press the seams toward the center.

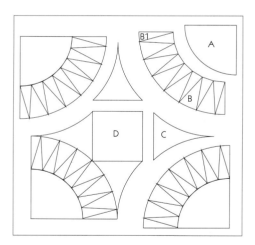

Fig. 5-23.

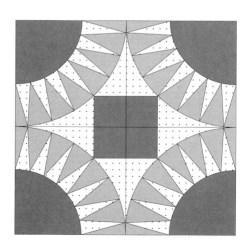

Whig's Defeat Sunburst.

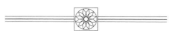

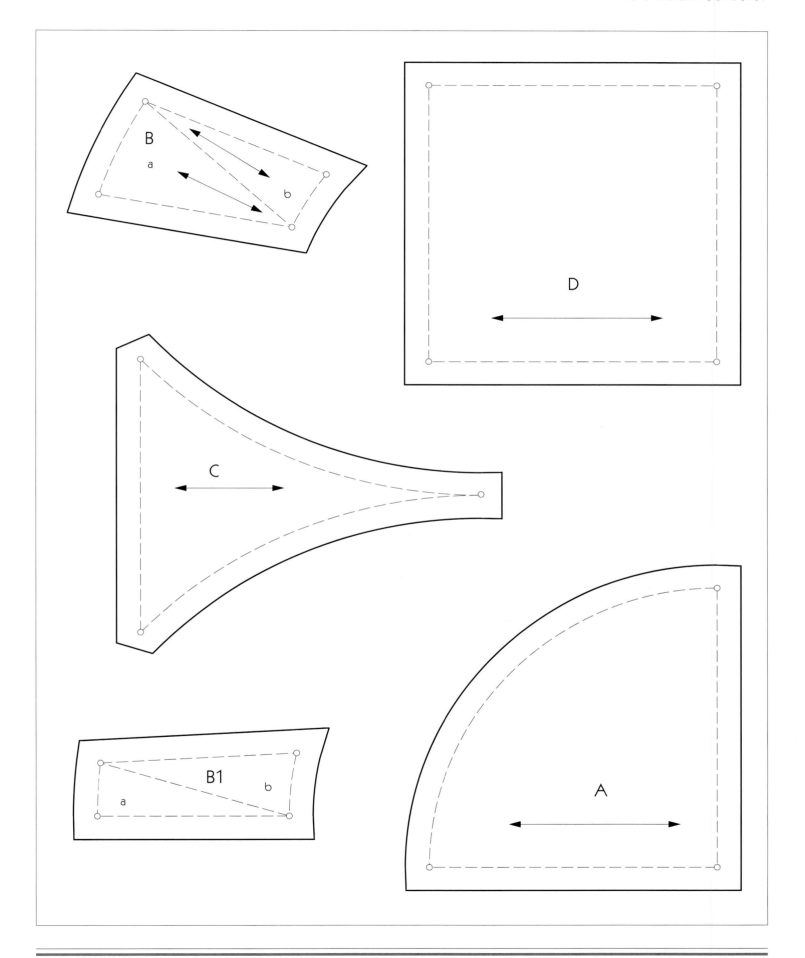

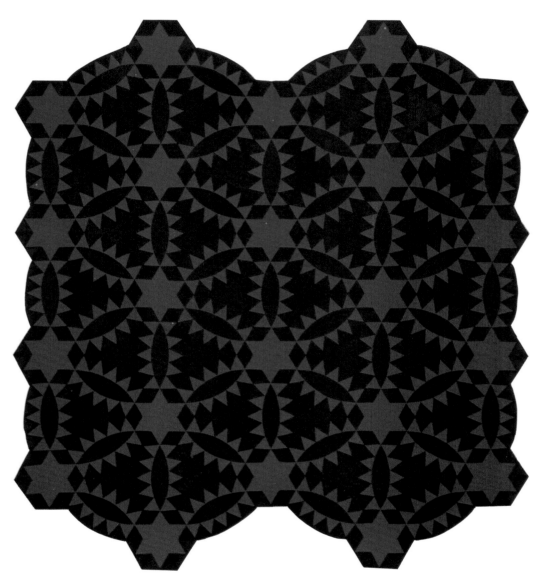

Plate 5-5. Candy Dish. 52" x 58".
Hot pink and black cotton. Unquilted.

CANDY DISH

Block size: approximately 11¼" X 13"

To determine the *width* of a single row of rings, multiply the number of rings by 11¼". Add to that total 5" for the two exterior arcs needed to complete the row. To make the sides and corners of the quilt identical, the number of rings in a horizontal row are always divisible by two. To determine the *length* of a single row of rings, multiply the number of rings by 13". The number of rings in a vertical row can be any even or odd number over two.

First determine the quilt width. In the illustration the quilt top's horizontal rows are four rings wide. The first and second rows look slightly different because the rows are staggered. The first row is just four rings. The second row is four rings and two exterior arcs. To determine the width, multiply four by 11¼" resulting in 45" plus 5" for the exterior arcs equals 50" wide. The second measure is the quilt length. The length of the quilt is measured from the longest points on the curved edge. Each ring is measured from the middle of a star to the middle of the next star. The illustration is four rings long or 4 times 13" equals 52". *(Fig. 5-24)*

The set of the blocks makes one edge almost straight, while the other edge is gently curved. In this layout the straighter edges are considered the sides of the quilt, and they would hang on the sides of the bed. The layout can be switched to make the straighter edges the top and bottom of the quilt and the gently curved edges the quilt sides. *(Fig. 5-25)*

There are 6 striplate pieces in each arc.
The strips are cut
    3" for side a
    2½" for side b
Approximately 18 striplates can be cut
    along each 45" seam.

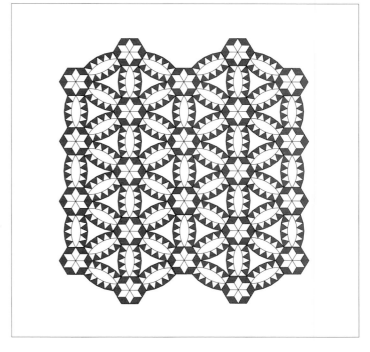

Fig. 5-24.

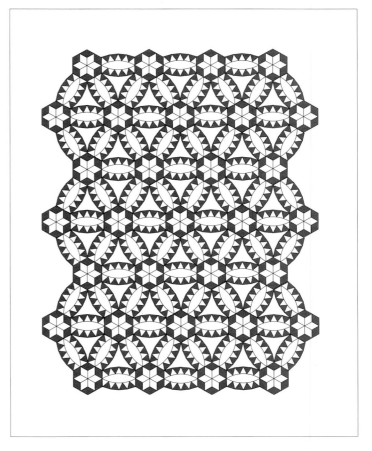

Fig. 5-25.

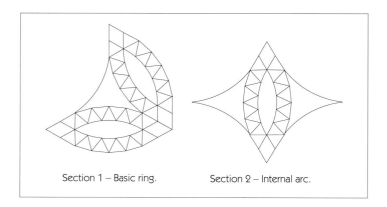

Section 1 – Basic ring.   Section 2 – Internal arc.

Fig. 5-26.

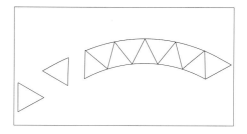

Fig. 5-27.

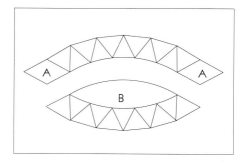

Fig. 5-28.

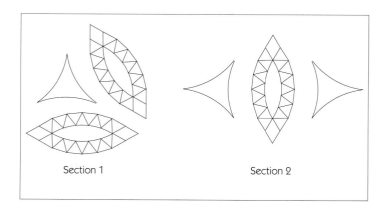

Section 1   Section 2

Fig. 5-29.

Construction Notes

Candy Dish is a variation of a pattern called Diamond Wedding Ring. It is based on the hexagon star, and the block center is a curved triangle. Candy Dish, like other Wedding Ring variations, is not a true block pattern. The quilt top is constructed from ring sections rather than identical blocks. The complexity of the finished pattern belies the simple set. The illustration highlights the two basic ring sections.

The basic ring, section 1, makes both the edges and body of the quilt. It is the most frequently used ring section in the quilt. It is made of four arcs, two ellipses, and a center. *(Fig. 5-26)*

The internal arc, section 2, is used in the body of the quilt as a bridge between the basic arc sections. The number of internal arcs depends on the quilt size, but as a rule basic ring sections outnumber internal arcs, about eight to one. The internal arc section is made from two arcs and one ellipse.

<u>Block Directions</u>
- Piece the arcs. Like Friendship, Candy Dish does not use half pieces on the arc ends. To piece the arcs, join five striplate pieces. For the final piece in each arc use the sixth striplate piece. Separate side a and b, by ripping the seam between the pieces. Discard side b. Press side a to remove the crease along the seam line and join it to the correct end of the arc. *(Fig. 5-27)*
- Stitch an arc to one side of each ellipse, piece B. When possible press the seam towards the ellipse.
- Before stitching the second arc to the ellipse add a diamond to each arc end. Join one diamond A to each end of the arc. This piece will make the six pointed star at the intersection of the rings. Press the seams toward the diamond. *(Fig. 5-28)*
- Stitch the second arc to the ellipse. Press the seams toward the ellipse. This ellipse and arc unit is used to make the ring sections.
- For ring section 1, join two ellipse and arc units to a center piece C. For the internal arc section 2, join one arc and ellipse unit to two centers, piece C's. *(Fig. 5-29)*

Joining the Ring Sections

    The ring sections are joined in rows and the rows are stitched together to make the quilt. The most difficult piecing in this pattern is the hexagon star. It is important that the quilt is pieced in a way that allows the star to be made in two halves, with a single center seam. To do that requires the quilt be constructed on diagonal rows of ring sections. The diagonal set is easy and logical. The rows are based on groups or units of three-ring sections. The same unit is repeated over and over for the entire quilt. The units are joined with internal arc sections and single centers, piece C. Notice the quilt is edged with completed hexagon stars. These extra pieces are made from template A and A1.

- Join three basic ring sections (section 1) as illustrated. *(Fig. 5-30)* This unit will make the upper right-hand corner of the quilt.
- Add the correct number of piece A's and E's to the corner section. Stitch two piece E's to each piece A. When joining the A-E units needed for the hexagon stars, some of the E pieces will be matched to the striplate piece D. *(Fig. 5-31)* Piece D has a slightly curved edge to join the block center, while the edges of E are straight to maintain a straight edge on the quilt. Line up the pieces as evenly as possible, make sure the curved edge of piece D does not extend beyond piece E. Sew a straight seam, not curved. The seam allowance will not be an exact ¼" at the outer edge of piece D. This is all right. The small error will not distort the finished quilt.
- Make another two identical units of three basic ring sections. Place the two units on a table as illustrated. To join the two units of ring sections requires an additional center piece. Stitch piece C to the upper unit as shown. Then join the units together to make a row. Notice that in this row the upper right-hand unit of three rings is the top edge of the quilt. Join the additional A-E units to make the quilt edge. *(Fig. 5-32, page 60)*
- Make another two units of three basic ring sections. In the illustration, notice the right and left units are on the sides on the quilt. The right-hand unit is reversed from the left unit, to make the quilt side. The units are joined by an internal arc section (section 2). Join the additional A-E units to make the quilt edge. *(Fig. 5-33, page 60)*
- In the quilt set used for the illustration the next row is a duplicate of the row made in step 8. *(Fig. 5-34, page 60)*
- The lower left-hand corner is a duplicate of the corner previously made.
- Pin the rows together securely pinning the matches and machine stitch the diagonal seam.

Fig. 5-30.

Fig. 5-31.

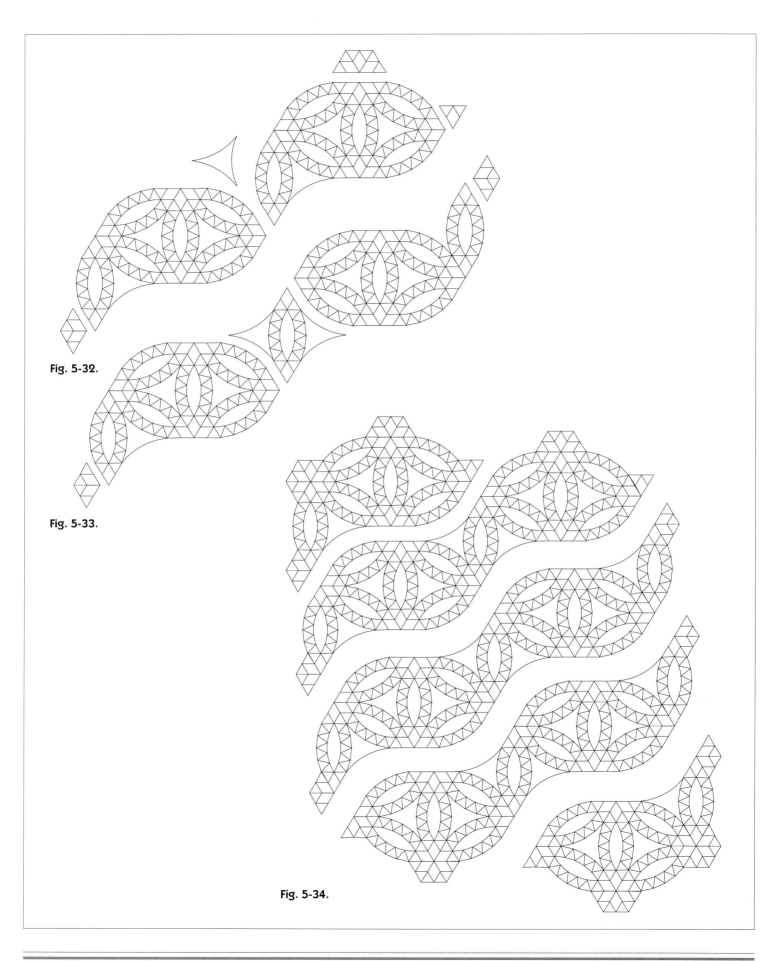

Fig. 5-32.

Fig. 5-33.

Fig. 5-34.

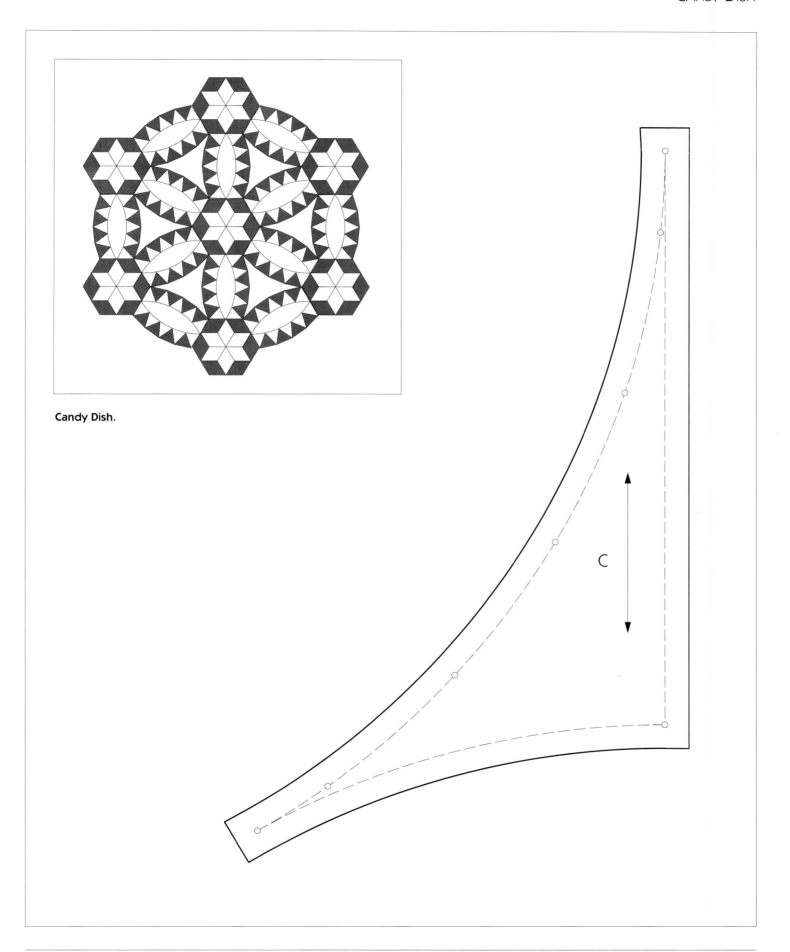

Candy Dish.

C

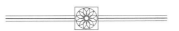

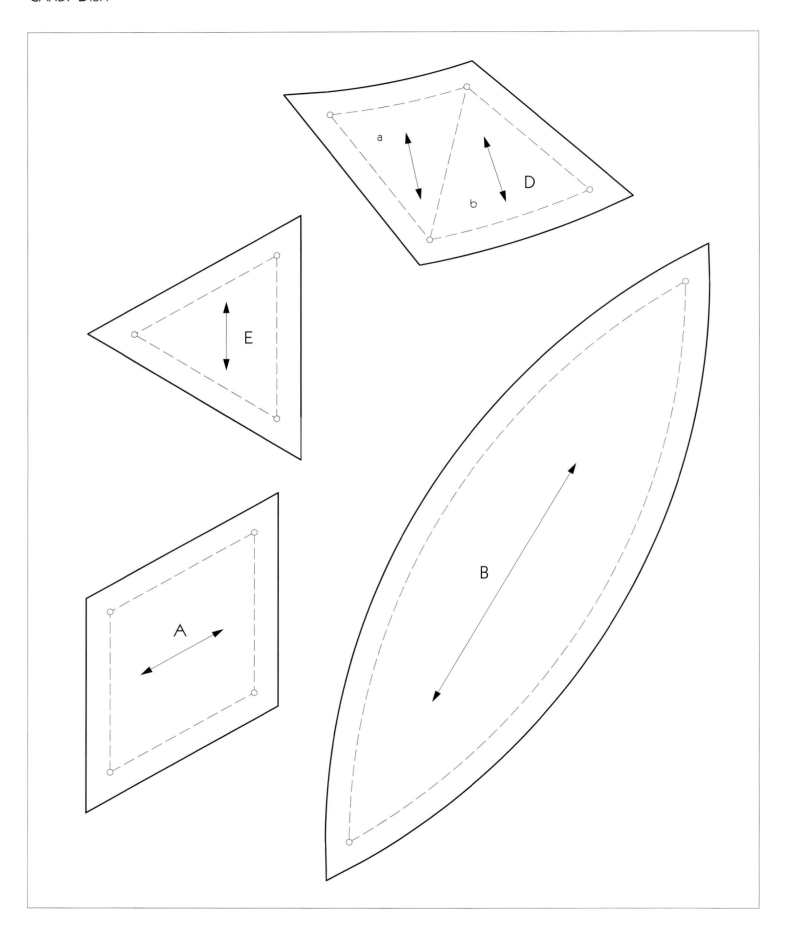

Plate 5-6. Sunflower Variation. 40" x 40".
Assorted coral, blue and green prints, cotton. Half and quarter blocks
are used in the Rainbow set. Unquilted.

Plate 5-7. Sunflower Variation. 28" x 28".
Navy mini dot and white cotton. Half and quarter blocks are set in
rows to give the Clamshell effect. With navy border. Unquilted.

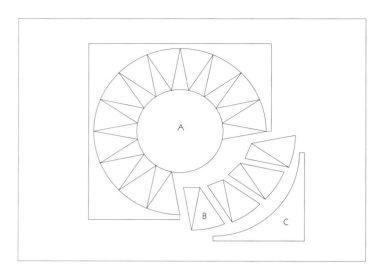

Fig. 5-35.

SUNFLOWER VARIATION

Block size: 6½" and 9"

There are 16 striplate pieces in each circle.

The strips for the 6½" block are cut

    2¼" for side a

    2" for side b

Approximately 20 striplates can be cut along each 45" seam.

The strips for the 9" block are cut

    2¾" for side a

    2¼" for side b

Approximately 14 striplates can be cut along each 45" seam.

Block Directions

• Piece the circle by joining 16 striplate pieces B. *(Fig. 5-35)*

• Join 1 piece A and 4 piece C's to the striplate circle to make the block. *(Fig. 5-36)*

Fig. 5-36.

Sunflower.

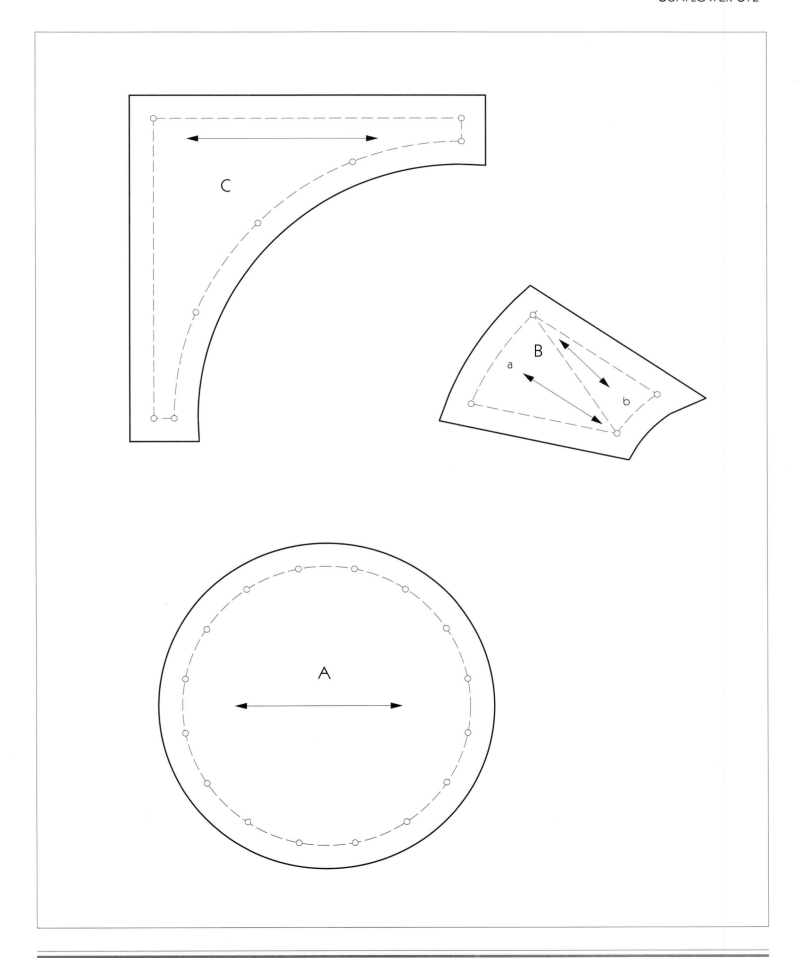

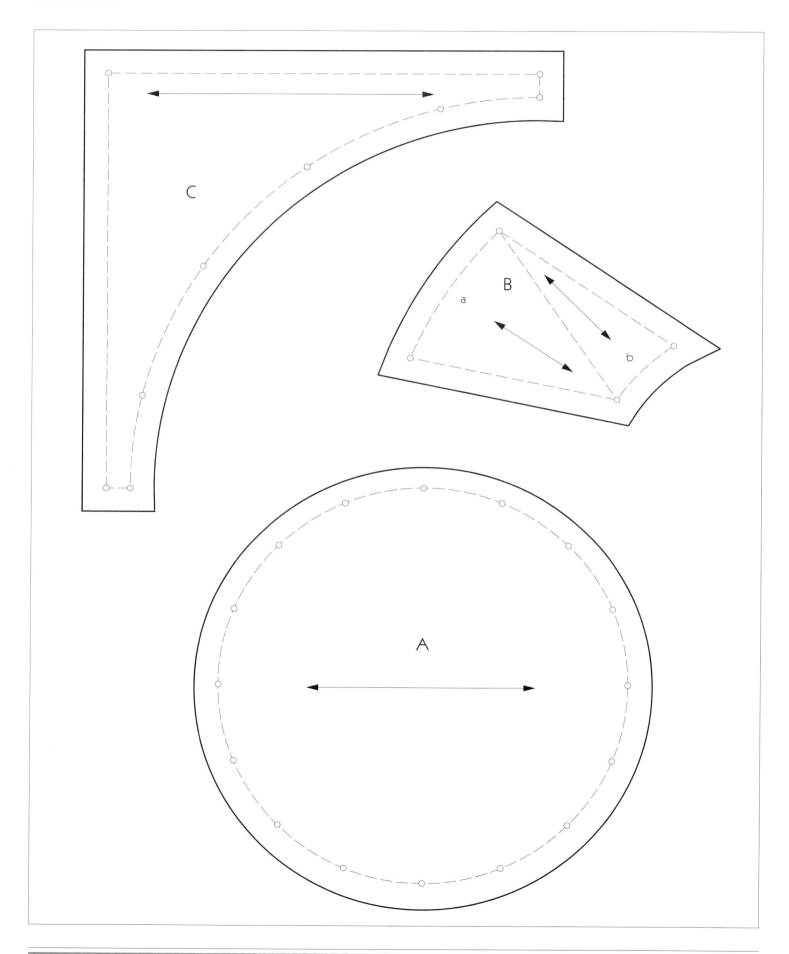

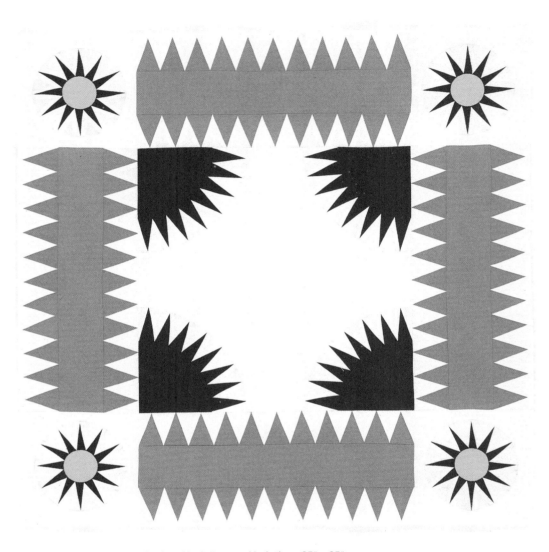

Plate 5-8. New York Beauty Variation. 25" x 25".
Cream, Turkey red, sage, and gold cottons. A single block bordered
with sashing. Unquilted.

Plate 5-9. New York Beauty Variation. 28½" x 28½".
Turkey red, gold, and cream cottons. A single block set with sashing.
The sashing corners are made from quarters of the block. To make the
corner sawteeth and sashing sawteeth match, narrow the center band
of the sashing to finish 2" wide. Bordered with chevroned diamonds.

New York Beauty Variation

Block size: 13¾"

There are 9 striplate pieces in each arc or 36 in each block.

The strips are cut

2¼" for side a

2" for side b

Approximately 16 striplates can be cut along each 45" seam.

Sashing size: 5¾" wide x 13¾" long

There are 12 striplate pieces on each side of the sashing or

24 in each sashing strip.

The strips are cut

2½" for side a

2½" for side b

Approximately 16 striplates can be cut along each 45" seam.

Sashing block size: 5¾" square

There are 12 striplate pieces in each circle of the

sashing block.

The strips are cut

2½" for side a

1¾" for side b

Approximately 21 striplates can be cut along each 45" seam.

Block Directions

- Piece the arcs by joining 9 striplate piece B's. Use template B1 to cut the arc ends.
- Stitch the arcs to piece A to make the arc corner. Press the seams away from the arc. *(Fig. 5-37)*
- Join the arc corners to the center C. Press the seams toward the center.

Sashing Directions

- Piece the sawtooth strips by joining 12 striplate piece G's. Use template G1 to make the strip ends. *(Fig. 5-38)*
- Rotary cut a strip 2¾" wide by 14¼" long for the center strip of the sashing. Stitch the sawtooth strips to the center strip. Press the seams toward the center.

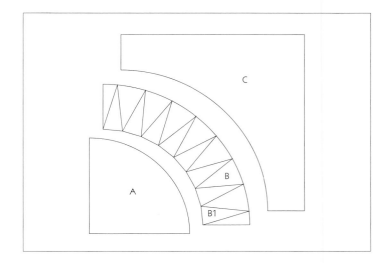

Fig. 5-37.

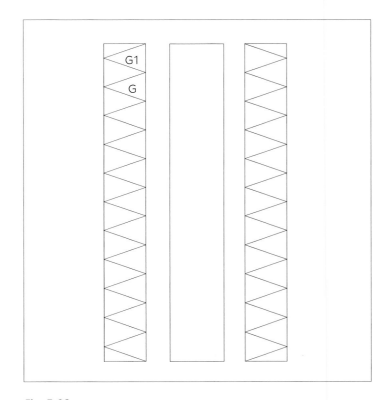

Fig. 5-38.

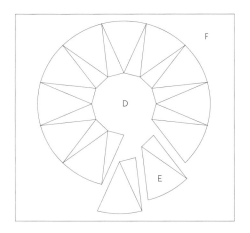

Fig. 5-39.

Fig. 5-40.

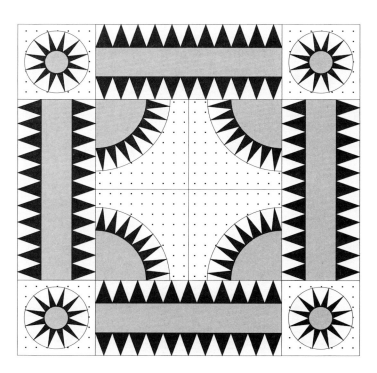

New York Beauty.

Sashing Block Directions

• Piece the circle by joining 12 striplate piece E's. *(Fig. 5-39)*

• Join piece D's and 4 piece F's to the striplate circle to make the sashing block. *(Fig. 5-40)*

Quilt Set Directions

In the traditional set the blocks are framed on all sides with sashing and the sashing makes the edge of the quilt. Occasionally additional arcs are added to the edges of the straight set to make a curved edge. Straight set and diagonal sets are both common. *(Fig. 5-41)*

Fig. 5-41.

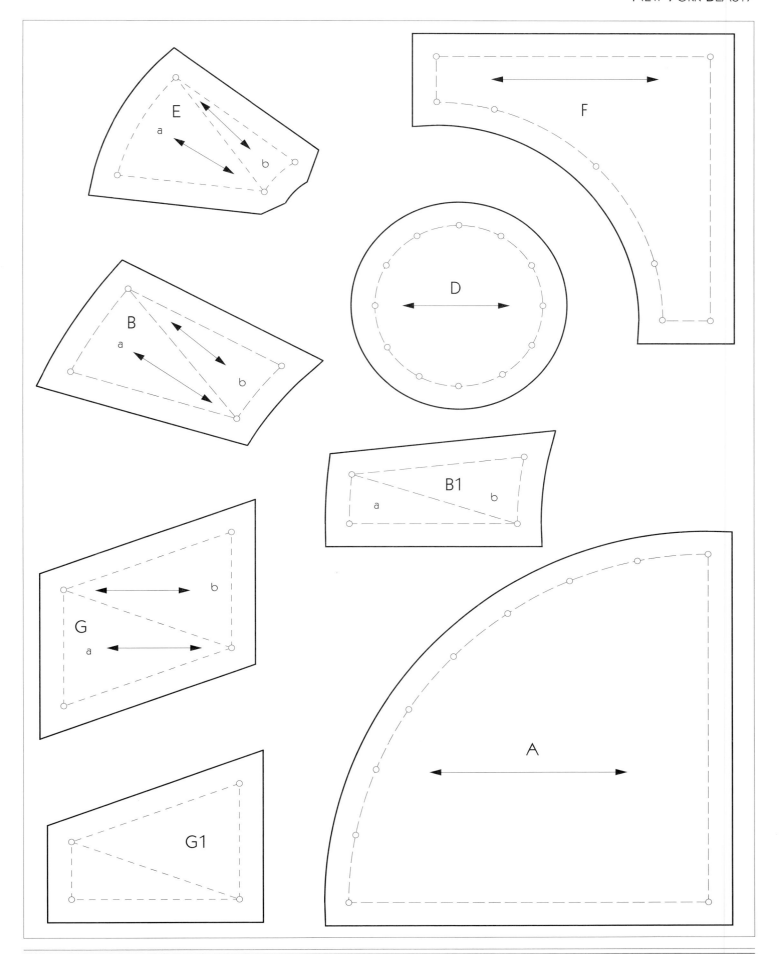

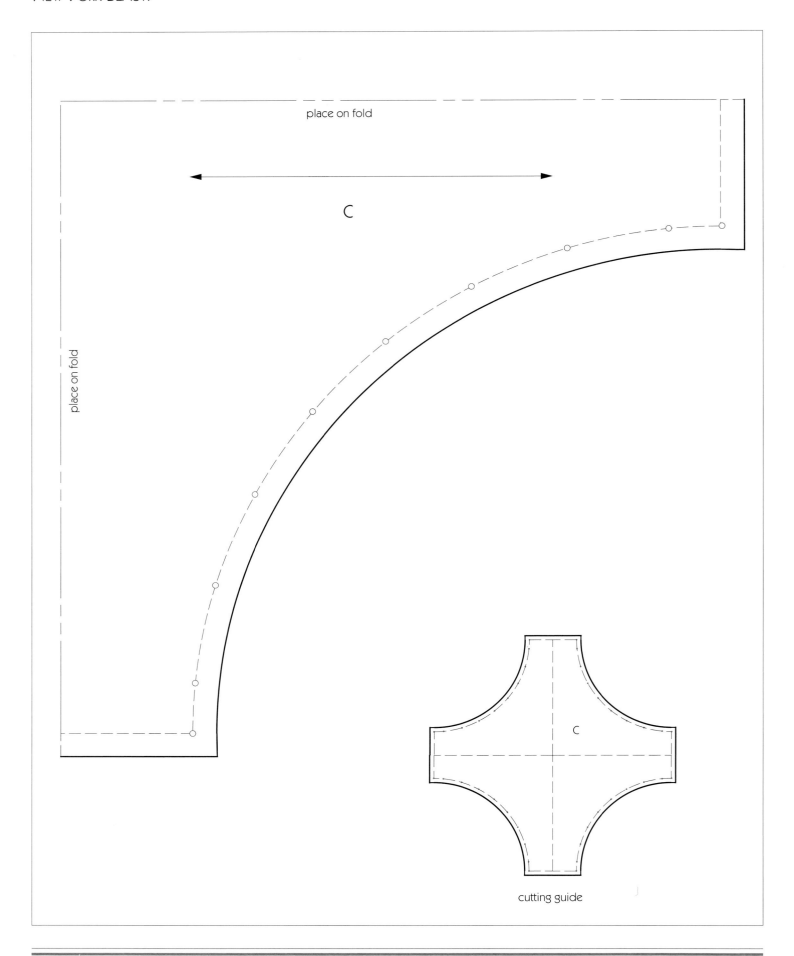

place on fold

place on fold

C

C

cutting guide

Plate 5-10. Wagon Wheel. 24" x 24".
Turquoise and black cotton. A single block bordered with a triple border and Nine-Patch set squares.

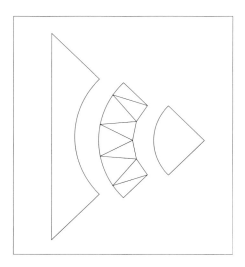

Fig. 5-42.

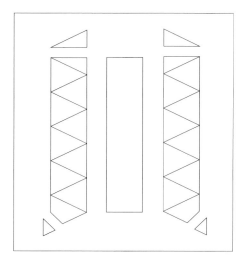

Fig. 5-43.

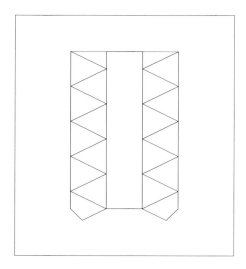

Fig. 5-44. Finished strip.

Wagon Wheel

Block size: Approximately 16"

There are 5 striplate piece F's in each arc or 20 in each block.

The strips are cut

2½" for side a

2¼" for side b

Approximately 20 striplates can be cut along each 45" seam.

There are 5 striplate piece H's in each straight strip or 40 in each block.

20 pieces are cut with the template right side up. 20 pieces are mirror images and are cut with the template wrong side up.

The strips are cut

2¾" for side a and b.

Approximately 18 striplates can be cut along each 45" seam.

Arc Directions

• Piece the arcs by joining 5 striplate piece F's. Use template F1 to cut the arc ends.

• Stitch the arcs to piece G to make the arc corner. *(Fig. 5-42)* Press the seams away from the arc.

• Join the arc corners to the block edge E. Press the seams toward the edge.

Straight Strip Directions

• Piece the straight strips by joining 5 striplate piece H's. Make eight straight strips, four from each set of twenty.

• The straight strips are sets of mirror images. Before cutting the strips to size, place four strips on the right hand side, four strips on the left hand side. Lay out the strips as they appear in the illustration. *(Fig. 5-43)* The lower piece in each strip is dark colored and the upper piece is light colored. The strips almost perfectly fit the space and the strip ends can be cut using templates H1 and H2. H1 is used to cut the upper light piece. H2 is used to cut the lower dark piece. Remember the strips are mirror images.

• Stitch the straight strips to the center strip C. Press the seams toward the center. *(Fig. 5-44)*

Block Directions

- Join two piece A's to a piece B four times to make the four units of the center block. *(Fig. 5-45)*
- Stitch the A-B units to the straight strips.
- Stitch a piece D to the other end of the straight strips.
- Join the four straight strips, to make an X shape.
- Inset the arc units to complete the block.

Fig. 5-45.

Wagon Wheel.

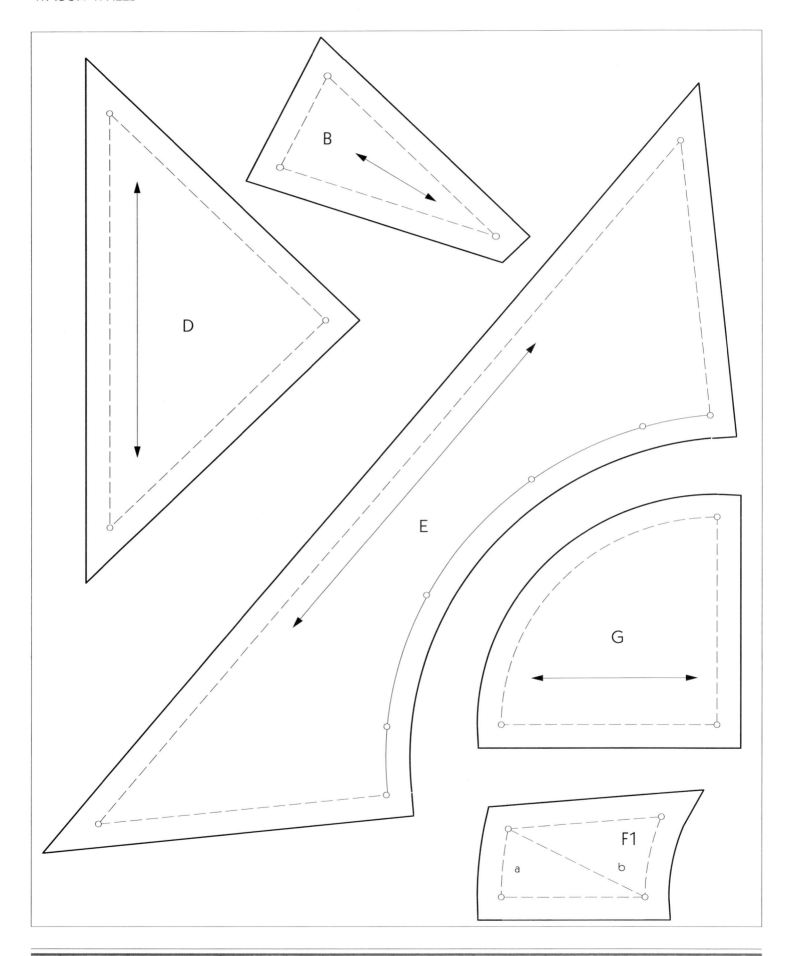

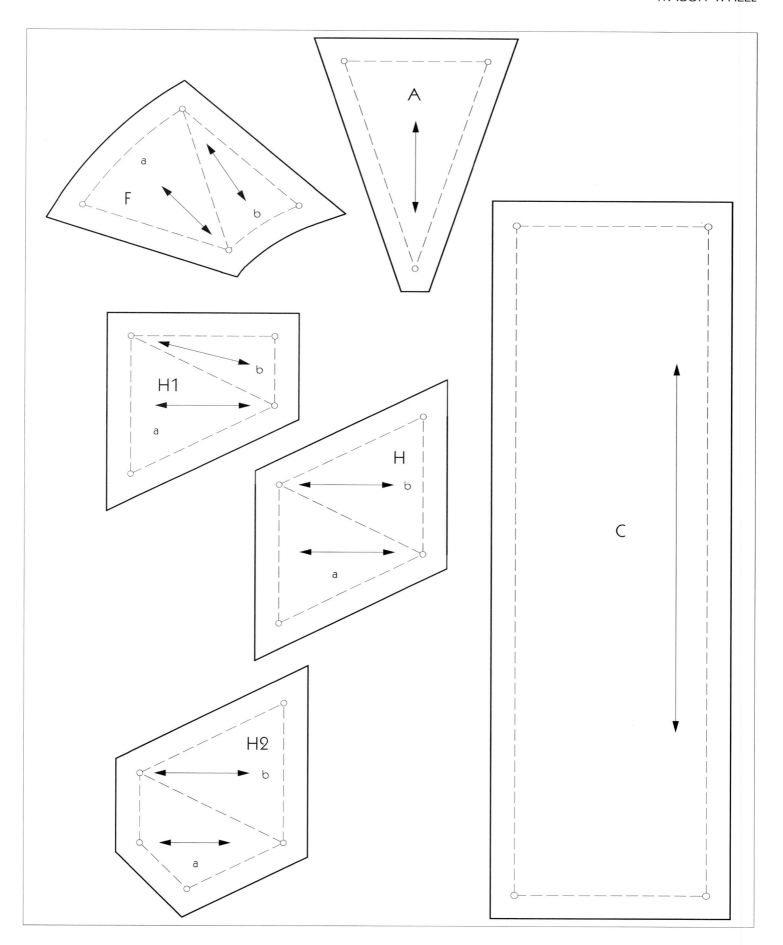

Plate 5-11. Madras Interchange. 56" x 56".
Hot pink, turquoise, and black cottons. The body of the quilt is four blocks. The borders are a variation using the center and inner sections of the basic block. The border corners are Sunflower pattern. Machine quilted. Owned by Fairfield Processing.

MADRAS INTERCHANGE

Block size: 19"

There are 9 striplate piece C's in each corner arc or 36 in each block.

The strips are cut

2¾" for side a

2" for side b

Approximately 12 striplates can be cut along each 45" seam.

There are 12 striplate piece D's in each quarter of the block or 48 in each block.

The strips are cut

2¼" for side a

2" for side b

Approximately 12 striplates can be cut along each 45" seam.

The pattern offers two center block versions, choose one.

An Eight-pointed Sunflower – pieces E, F, and G.

There are 8 striplate piece F's in each center block.

The strips are cut

2½" for side a

1¾" for side b

Approximately 20 striplates can be cut along each 45" seam.

Sawtooth Center – pieces J and J1.

There are 16 striplate piece J's in each center block.

The strips are cut

2" wide for side a and b.

Approximately 12 striplates can be cut along each 45" seam.

BLOCK CENTERS

• Complete the block centers before beginning the remaining portions of the block.

SUNFLOWER CENTER

• Piece the circle by joining 8 striplate piece F's.

• Join pieces E and 4 piece G's to the striplate circle to make the block. *(Fig. 5-46)* Set the sunflower center aside; it will be used to complete the block.

SAWTOOTH CENTER

• Join four piece J's to form one quarter of the center block. Use template J1 to trim the strip ends. See the illustration. Do not join the four pieces to make the center square. The quarters will be joined to the block quarters before completing the block. *(Fig. 5-47)*

<u>Block Directions</u>

• Piece the corner arcs by joining 9 striplate piece C's. Use template C1 to cut the arc ends. *(Fig. 5-48)*

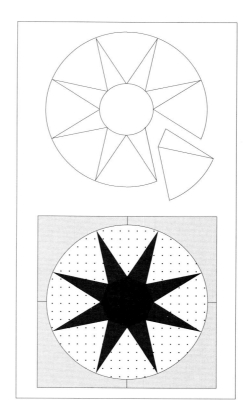

Fig. 5-46.

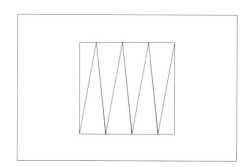

Fig. 5-47.

Fig. 5-48. Corner.

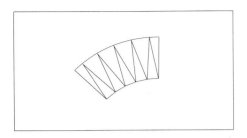

Fig. 5-49. Quarter arc D.

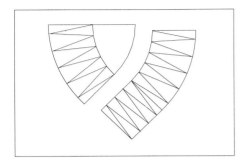

Fig. 5-50.

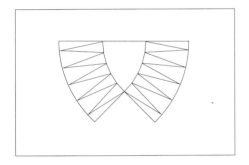

Fig. 5-51.

- Stitch the arcs to piece B. Press the seams away from the arc.
- Join each arc to two block corners I. Press the seams toward the edge. Set the corner arcs aside; they will be used to complete the block.
- Piece the quarter arcs by joining 6 piece D's. *(Fig. 5-49)* Use template D1 to cut the arc ends.

USING THE SAWTOOTH CENTER
- Lay out the two arcs, a sawtooth center, and piece A as illustrated. Stitch one arc to piece A. *(Fig. 5-50)*
- Stitch the other arc to the sawtooth center, then join the unit to piece A. Join piece H to the left side of the block quarter made in the previous steps.

USING THE SUNFLOWER CENTER
- Lay out the two arcs, and piece A as illustrated. Stitch the right and left arcs to piece A. *(Fig. 5-51)* Go to next step.
- Join piece H to the left side of the block quarter made in the previous steps. *(Fig. 5-52)*
- Join the block quarters to make the inner block. If you chose the Sunflower center, insert the center block at this time. *(Fig. 5-53)*
- Finish the block by joining the corner arcs made in the steps above.

Fig. 5-52. Join four quarters and add corners.

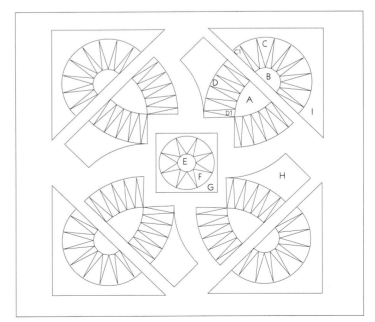

Fig. 5-53. After the four quarters are sewn together inset the center block.

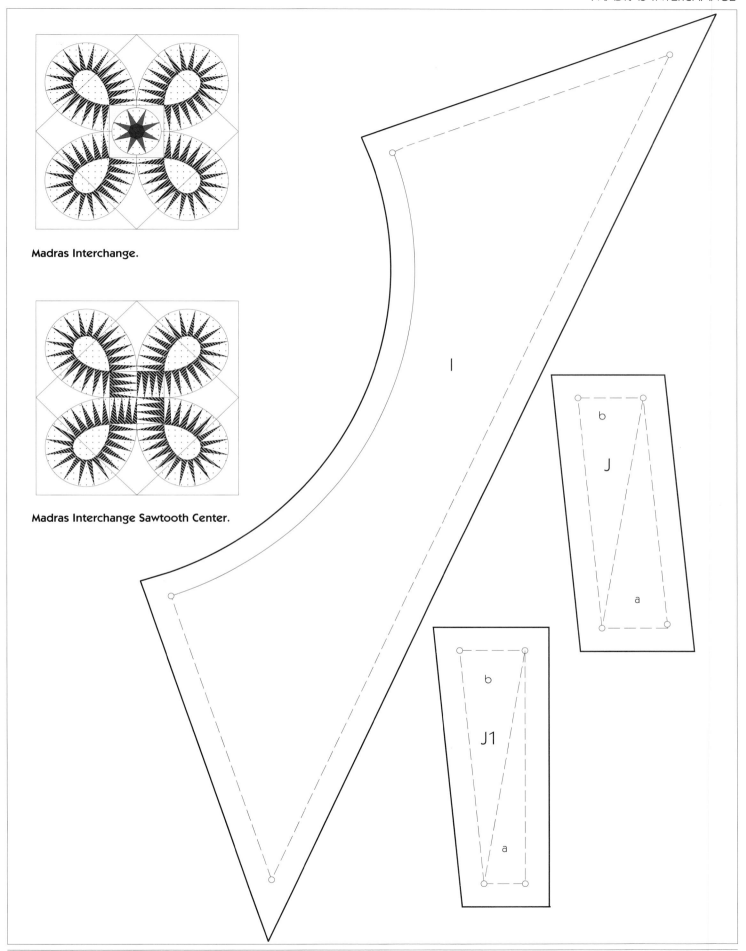

Madras Interchange.

Madras Interchange Sawtooth Center.

I

J

b

a

J1

b

a

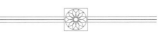

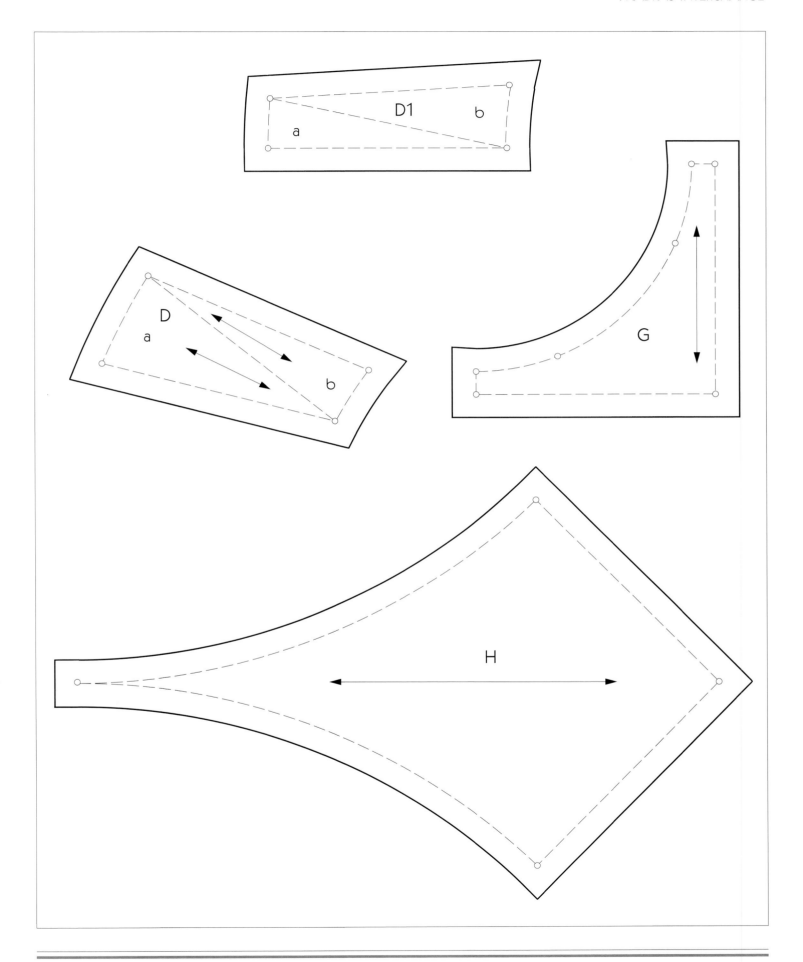

Plate 5-12. Rail through the Rockies. 70" x 92".
Red and white cotton. Diagonally set blocks. Machine quilted with tra-
punto. Privately owned.

RAIL THROUGH THE ROCKIES

This is a special pattern to me and has always been one of my favorites. I designed this pattern for my own quilt, RAIL THROUGH THE ROCKIES. This quilt won first place in its category at the AQS quilt show and was designated a Masterpiece Quilt by the National Quilting Association on August 10, 1992.

Block Size: 21"
There are two striplate arcs per block.
The inner striplate arc C has 12 striplate pieces or 48 in each block.
The strips are cut
    2" for side a
    1¾" for side b
Approximately 15 striplates can be cut along each 45" seam.

The outer striplate arc E has 17 striplate pieces or 68 in each block. The strips are cut 2" for side a and b.
Approximately 15 striplates can be cut along each 45" seam.

Sashing size: 6" x 21"
There are 29 striplate piece G's on each side of the sashing or 58 pieces in each sashing.
The strips are cut
    2" wide for side a and b.
Approximately 15 striplates can be cut along each 45" seam.

Sashing block size: 6"
There are 16 striplate pieces in each circle of the sashing block.
The strips are cut
    2¼" for side a
    1¼" for segment b
    1¾" for side c
Approximately 20 striplate pieces can be cut for each 45" strip b.

Block Directions
• Piece the inner striplate arcs by joining 12 striplate piece C's. Use template C1 to cut the arc ends.
• Piece the outer striplate arcs by joining 15 striplate piece E's. Use template E1 to cut the arc ends.
• Stitch piece B to corner piece A to form the corner unit. Press the seams away from the corner.
• Stitch striplate arc C to the corner unit. Press the seam toward the corner. Press carefully; do not distort piece C. (Fig. 5-54)

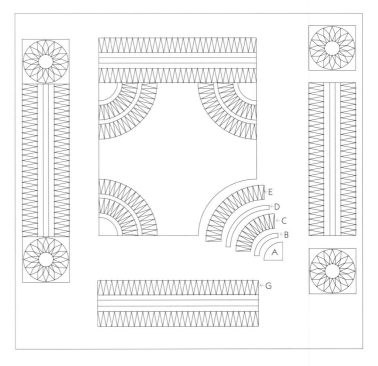

Fig. 5-54.

85

Fig. 5-55.

- Join piece D to the corner unit. Press the seam away from the corner. Press gently; do not distort piece D.
- Join striplate arc E to the corner unit. Press the seam toward the corner.
- Stitch the four corner units to the block center. Press the seams toward the center.

Sashing Directions
- Piece the sawtooth strips by joining 29 striplate piece G's. Use template G1 to make the strip ends.
- The center of the sashing strip is rotary cut. It is three pieces, each cut 1¼" wide by 21½" long. Join the three pieces to make a strip 2¾" wide by 21½" long. Press the seams away from the center.
- Stitch the sawtooth strips to the center strips. Press the seams toward the center.

Sashing Block Directions
- Piece the striplate circle by joining 16 piece I's.
- Join piece H and four piece J's to the striplate circle to make the sashing block. *(Fig. 5-55)*

Rail through the Rockies.

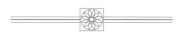

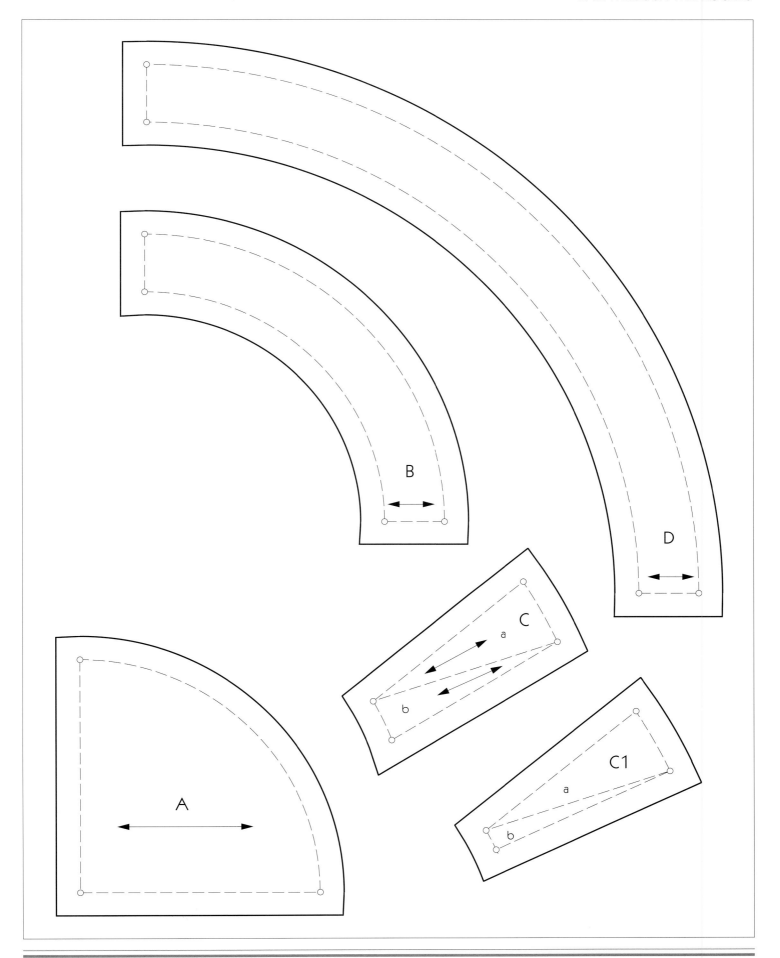

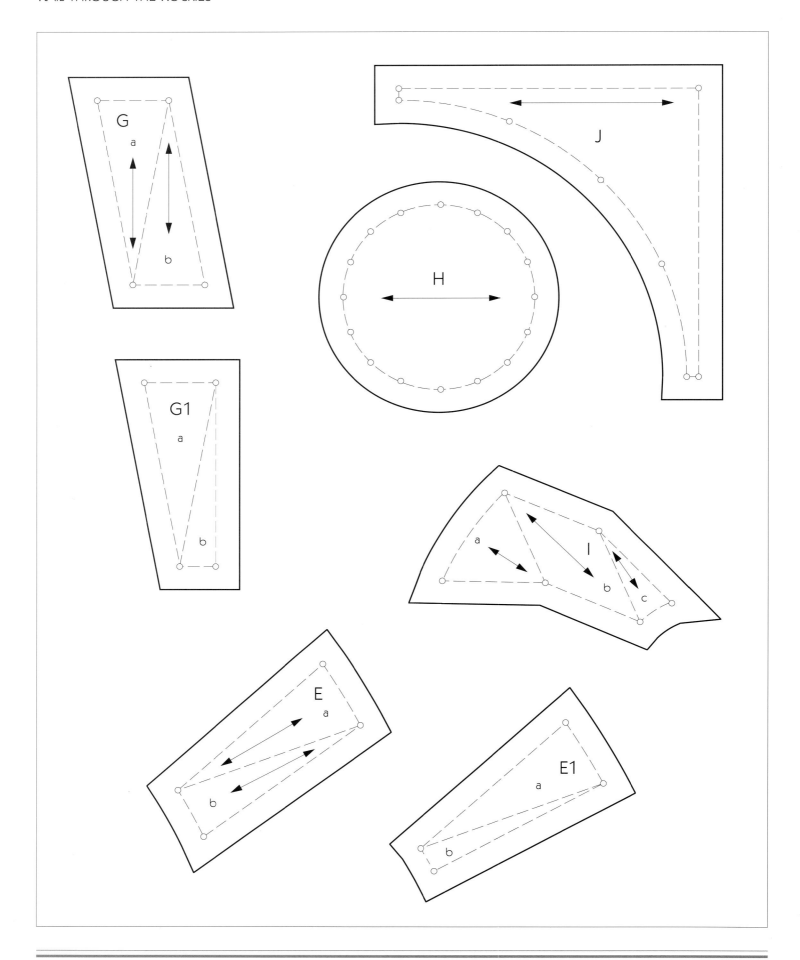

Plate 5-13. Kansas Sunflower. 29" x 29".
Navy, cream, and gold cottons. Four blocks with appliquéd bias trim.
Border with navy. Unquilted.

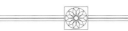

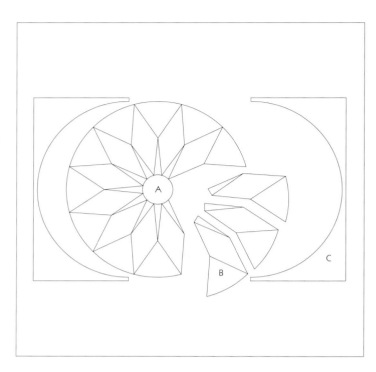

Fig. 5-56.

THREE-COLOR STRIPLATE PATTERNS

KANSAS SUNFLOWER

Block size: This pattern is offered in three sizes, 6½", 9½", and
12½" square.

There are twelve striplates in each block.

The strips for the 6½" block are cut
2½" for side a
1⅜" for segment b
1¾" for side c

Approximately 18 striplates can be cut from each 45" b strip.

The strips for the 9½" block are cut
3" for side a
1⅞" for segment b
1¾" for side c

Approximately 16 striplates can be cut from each 45" b strip.

The strips for the 12½" block are cut
4" for side a
2¼" for segment b
1¾" for side c

Approximately 12 striplates can be cut from each 45" b strip.

Block Directions

- Piece the striplate circle by joining 12 piece B's.
- Join piece A and four piece C's to the striplate circle to complete the block. *(Fig. 5-56)*

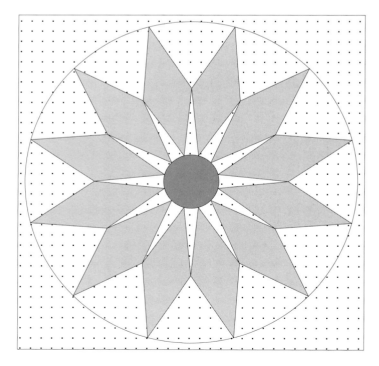

Kansas Sunflower.

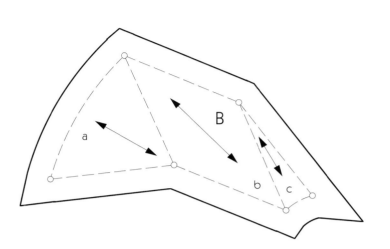

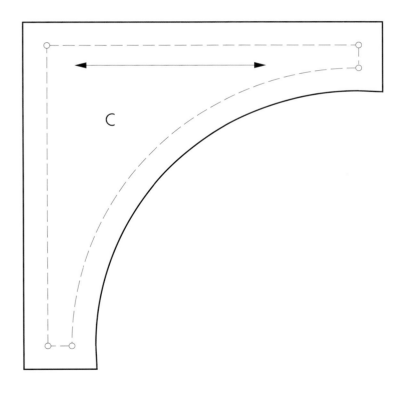

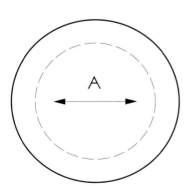

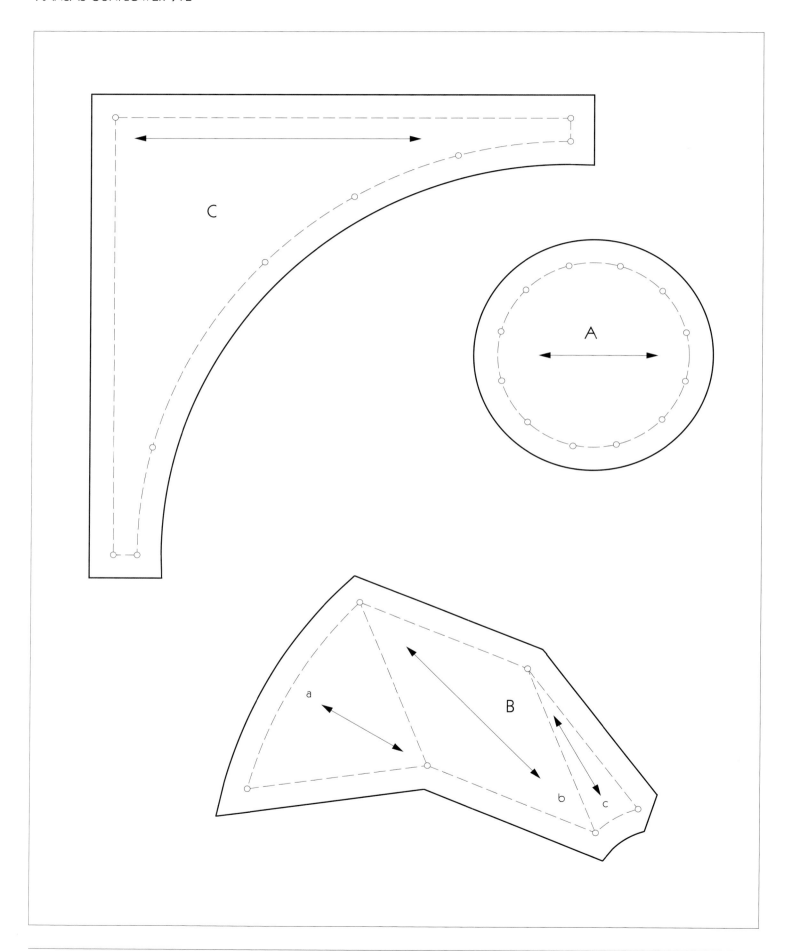

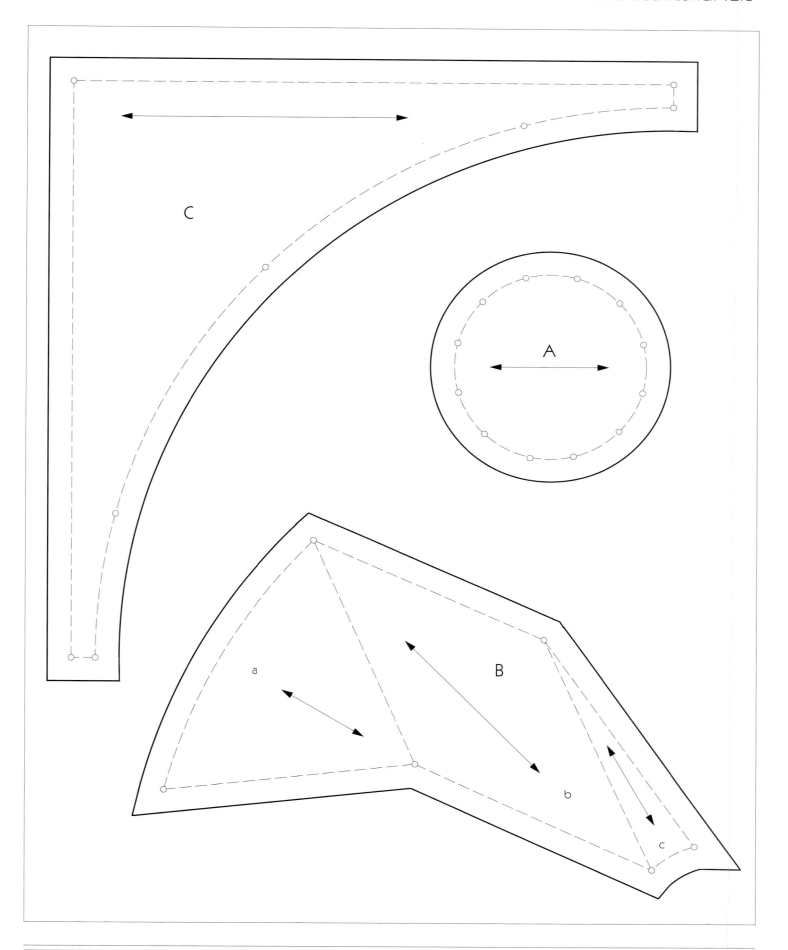

Plate 5-14. Setting Sun. 41" x 41".
Cream, green, and assorted gold and brown prints, cotton. Setting Sun
in Sunflower set. Five blocks with appliquéd leaves and stems. Bordered in gold. Unquilted.

Setting Sun

Block size: This pattern is offered in two sizes 8½" and
12½" square.

There are 16 striplates in each block.

The strips for the 8½" block are cut

2½" for side a

1½" for segment b

2" for side c

Approximately 18 striplates can be cut from each 45" b strip.

The strips for the 12½" block are cut

3¼" for side a

2" for segment b

2¼" for side c

Approximately 14 striplates can be cut from each 45" b strip.

Block Directions

- Piece the striplate circle by joining 16 piece B's.
- Join piece A and four piece C's to the striplate circle to complete the block. *(Fig. 5-57)*

Appliqué Directions

The appliqué Sunflower block is based on the 8½" block. The appliqué can be enlarged 147% to use with the 12½" block.

- To make the block, cut three 9" blocks, the color of piece C in the pieced sunflower. Join the three plain and one pieced block to make a 17½" block.
- Make 45" of 1" bias strips folded to finish ⅝" for the stems. Following the block illustration *(Fig. 5-58)*, appliqué the stems in place.
- Cut two leaf pieces. The pattern is the finished size; add ¼" seam allowances for hand appliqué. *(Fig. 5-59, page 96)* Appliqué the leaves to the block.

SET SUGGESTIONS

This quilt was inspired by an 1861 quilt by Carrie Persons. The blocks are set side by side divided by a narrow sashing strip that emulates the center stem. The blocks are off set a half block, requiring partial blocks on the top and bottom of the right-hand rows. The right-hand blocks are mirror images of the left-hand blocks. *(Fig. 5-60)*

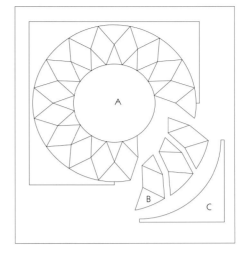

Fig. 5-57.

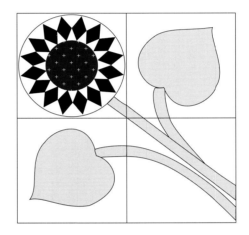

Fig. 5-58.

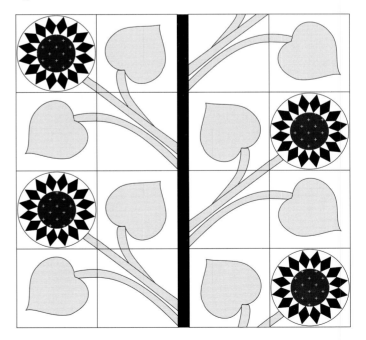

Fig. 5-60.

Fig. 5-59.

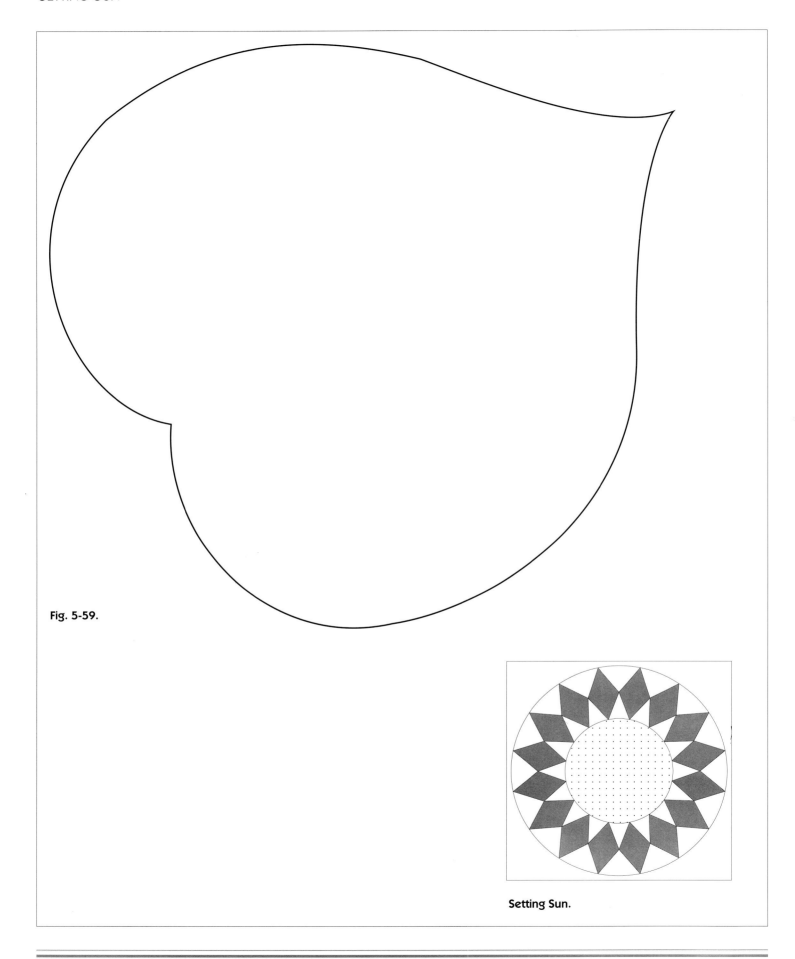

Setting Sun.

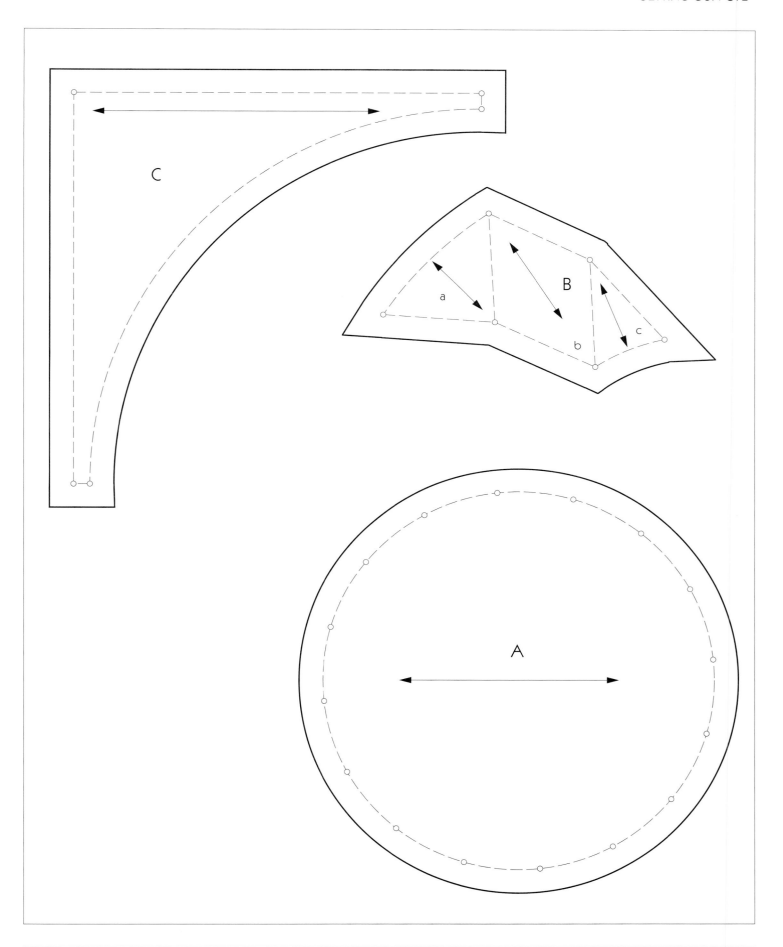

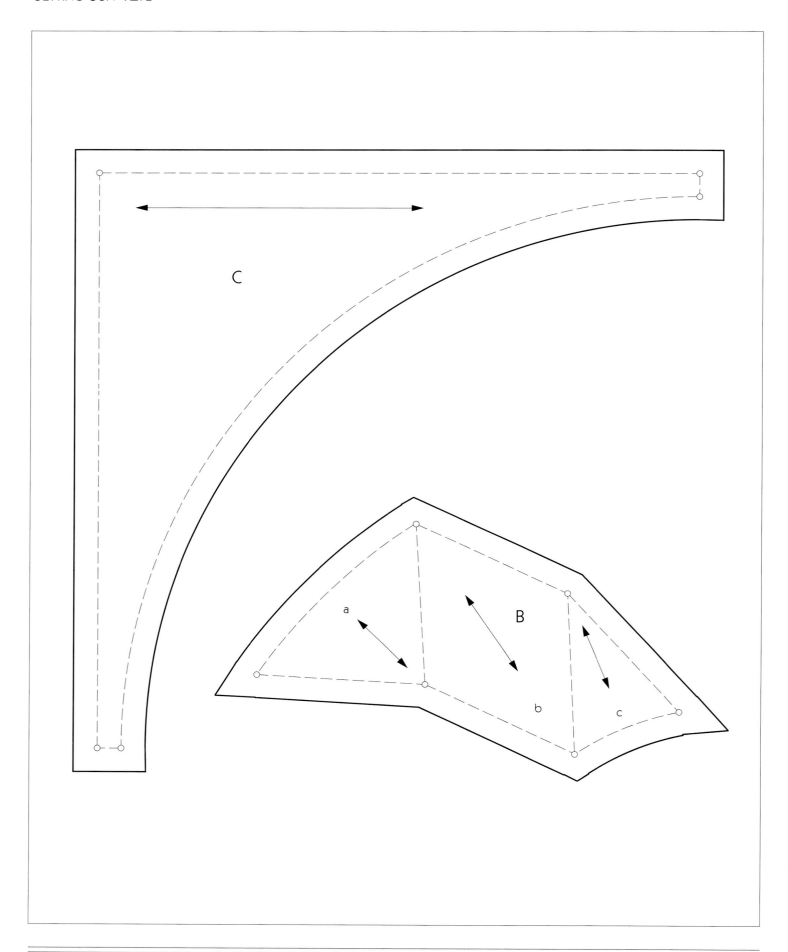

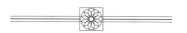
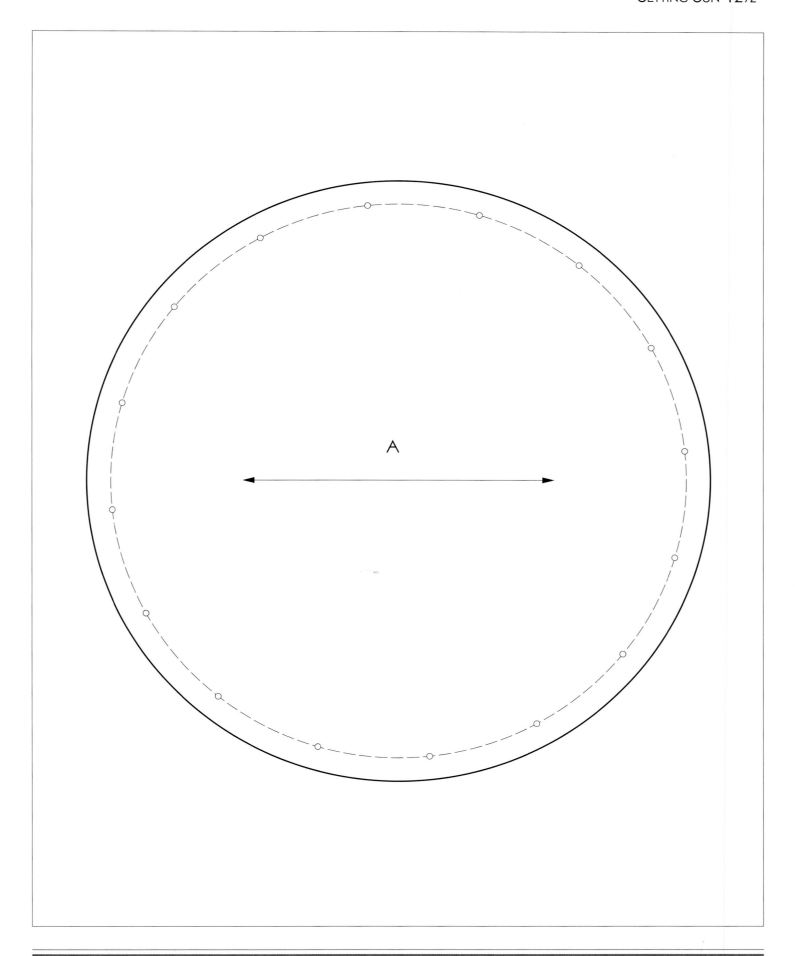

A

Plate 5-15. Whig's Defeat. 34" x 34".
Cream, brown, rust, and flax, all cotton. Four blocks, unquilted.

Plate 5-16. Whig's Defeat. 50" x 50".
Cream, two shades of green, and two shades of pink, all cotton. Four
block centers, with appliquéd sashing and borders. Machine quilted.

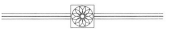

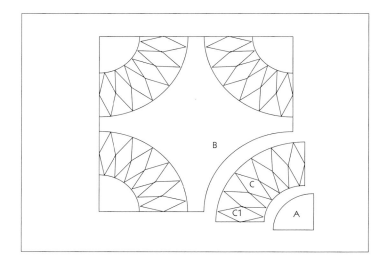

Fig. 5-61.

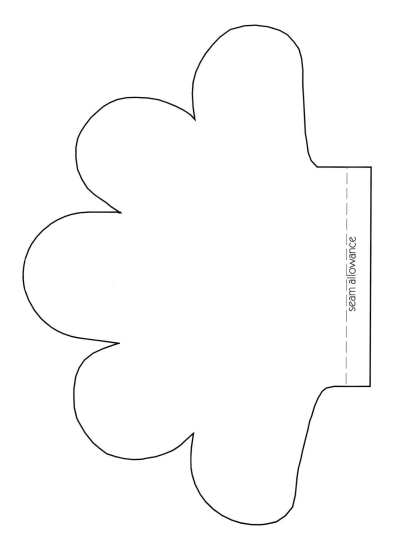

Fig. 5-62. Appliqué pattern.

seam allowance

WHIG'S DEFEAT

Block sizes: 9½" and 12"

There are 7 striplates in each arc or 28 in each block.

The strips for the 9½" block are cut

2¼" for side a

1¼" for segment b

1¾" for side c

Approximately 20 pieces can be cut from each 45" b strip.

The strips for the 12" block are cut

2½" for side a

1¼" for segment b

2" for side c

Please measure the pattern piece for strip b; it finishes slightly under 1" wide, cut a narrow 1¼" strip to compensate for the discrepancy.

Approximately 18 pieces can be cut from each 45" b strip.

<u>Block Directions</u>

• Piece the arcs, joining 6 striplate piece C's to make each arc. Divide the seventh striplate to complete the arc. Use template C1 to cut the arc ends. *(Fig. 5-61)*

• Join the arcs to the block corner A, to make the corner unit. Press the seam toward the corner.

• Stitch the corner units to the block center B. Press the seams toward the center.

<u>Appliqué Directions</u>

Traditionally Whig's Defeat is combined with an appliquéd design. The addition of the appliqué increases the 9½" block to approximately 13½". The appliqué can be enlarged 126% for use with the 12" block. *(Fig. 5-62)*

• To make the four appliqué corners cut two 7⅝" blocks, and then cut these diagonally to make a total of four triangles.

• Cut four leaf pieces. The pattern is the finished size; add ¼" seam allowances for hand appliqué. Appliqué one leaf to each corner of the block.

• Stitch the appliquéd corners on to the pieced block. The corners are slightly larger than the block to allow for the distortion that can occur when appliquéing. Stitch the corners in place and trim the excess fabric. *(Fig. 5-63, page 104)*

WEDDING RING VARIATION OF WHIG'S DEFEAT

This stunning variation of Whig's Defeat *(Fig. 5-64)* was inspired by a circa 1880 quilt by Dorinda Moody Slade. It uses the traditional corner appliqué and combines it with the Wedding Ring set. For a closer look at Dorinda's breathtaking work refer to *Pioneer Quiltmaker* by C. Davis.

The block size is approximately 17" based on the 9½" Whig's Defeat block.

Block Directions

- Piece the arcs, joining 6 striplate piece C's to make each arc. Divide the seventh striplate to complete the arc. Use template C1 to cut the arc ends.
- Join four arcs to four ellipses (E), to make the corner arcs. Press the seam toward the ellipse.
- Join corner B to each corner arc. Make four corners. Press the seams away from the striplate piecing.
- Stitch four arcs to the block center B. Press the seams toward the center. *(Fig. 5-65)*
- Rotary cut four rectangles, 5½" X 4½". Appliqué the leaf design on each rectangle. The appliqué pattern is the finished size; add ¼" seam allowances for hand appliqué.
- Stitch one appliquéd rectangle to each side of the center unit. Press the seams toward the rectangle.
- Join the corners to complete the block.

Fig. 5-63.

Fig. 5-65.

Fig. 5-64.

Plate 5-17. Whig's Defeat Wedding Ring Set. 15½" x 15½".
Cream, pink, yellow, and green, all cotton. A single block unquilted.

Whig's Defeat.

Whig's Defeat Appliqué.

Whig's Defeat Wedding Ring Variation.

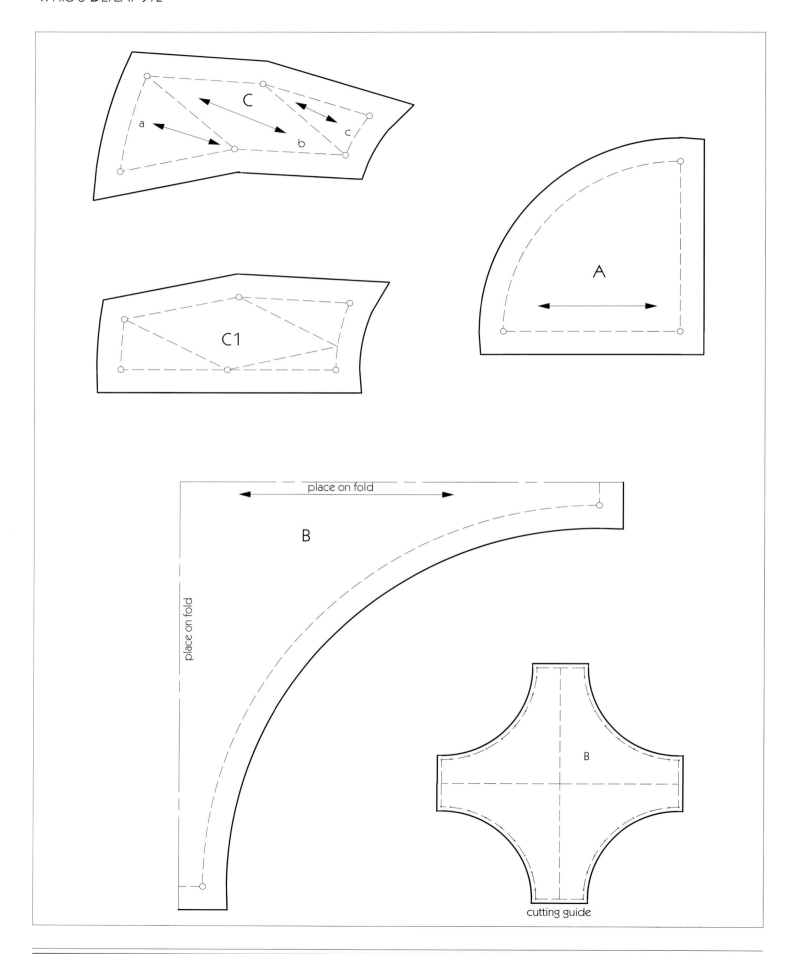

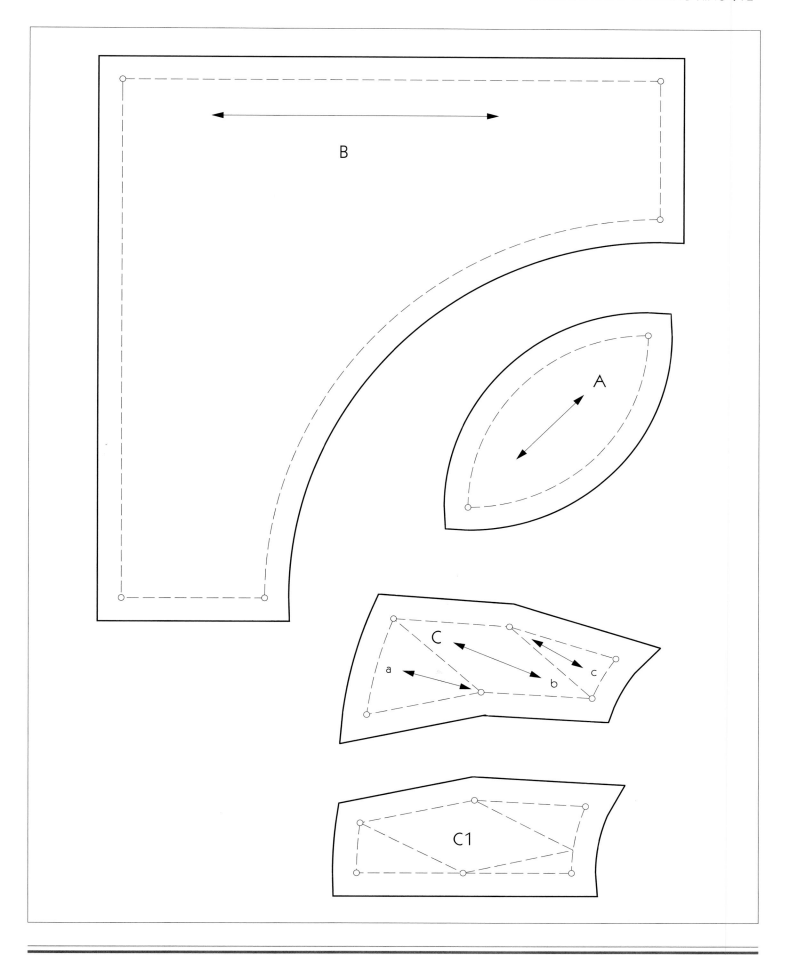

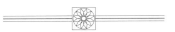

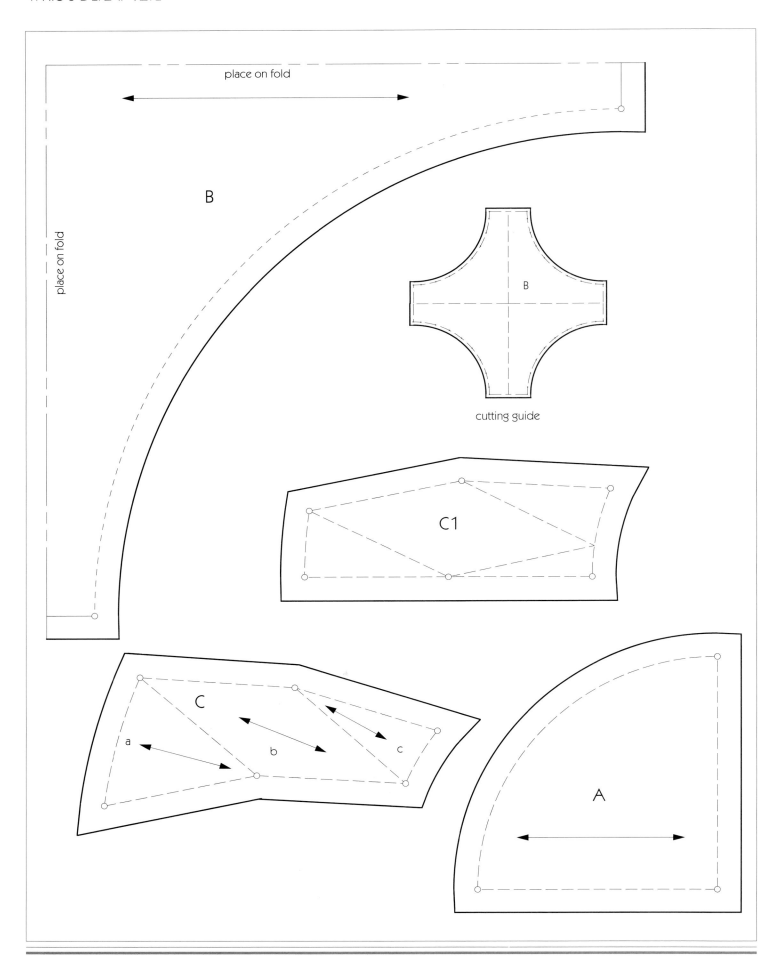

place on fold

place on fold

B

B

cutting guide

C1

C

a

b

c

A

Plate 5-18. Egyptian Lotus. 58" x 62".
Cream, red, gold, and green. A single block with appliquéd swag borders. Unquilted.

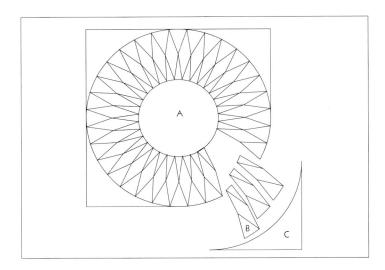

Fig. 5-66.

Fig. 5-67.

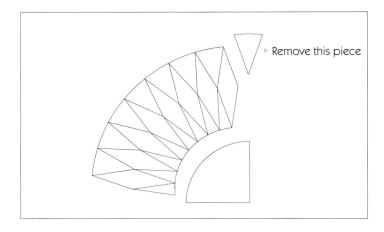

Fig. 5-68.

EGYPTIAN LOTUS

Block size: 15" and 18½"

There are 32 striplates in each 15" block.

The strips for the 15" block are cut

2¼" for side a

1½" for segment b

2" for side c

Approximately 12 striplates can be cut from each 45" b strip.

There are 36 striplates in each 18½" block.

The strips for the 18½" block are cut

3" for side a

1½" for segment b

1¾" for side c

Approximately 10 striplates can be cut from each 45" b strip.

Block Directions for Basic Circle Block

• Piece the striplate circle by joining 32 (15" block) or 36 (18½" block) piece B's. *(Fig. 5-66)*

• Join piece A and four piece C's to the striplate circle to complete the block.

Appliqué Directions

The appliquéd Egyptian Lotus block is based on the 15" block. The appliqué can be enlarged 123% to use it with the 18½" block. The block is made of one full circle and two arcs, plus an appliquéd urn, leaves, stems, and buds. The entire block is appliquéd, including the striplate circle and arcs. *(Fig. 5-67)*

Block size: 35" x 37½"

• Construct the 15" full circle block. Do not add the corner piece C's.

• Cut one block 36" x 40" to allow for any distortions that may occur during appliqué.

• Following the block illustration, make 72" of 1" bias strips folded to finish ½" for the stems. Appliqué the stems in place.

• Make two arcs of 8 striplate piece B's. Do not divide an additional striplate to complete the arc. The arc edges will be concealed under the appliqué. Remove the single outside edge piece to make both sides of the arc begin with the diamond pieces. *(Fig. 5-68)*

• Stitch the arcs to piece A1 to make a corner unit. This will not balance, but the unbalanced edges will be concealed by the appliqué. Appliqué the corner unit to the block.

• Cut the remaining appliqué pieces. The pattern is the finished size; add ¼" seam allowances for hand appliqué. Appliqué the design to the block.

<u>Set Directions</u>

This large block was inspired by a quilt called LOTUS FLOWER. The original was undated, but appeared in *The Romance of the Patchwork Quilt in America*, originally printed in 1935. Four large blocks will make the entire quilt top. I have included a 12" border swag designed to fit the four sides of the quilt. *(Fig. 5-69)*

Four blocks will total 70" x 75"; with the 12" borders the quilt will total 94" x 99". Five swags are used for each side of the quilt. The longer 15" swag is used on the 99" side, while the 14" swag is used on the 94" side.

Egyptian Lotus.

Fig. 5-69.

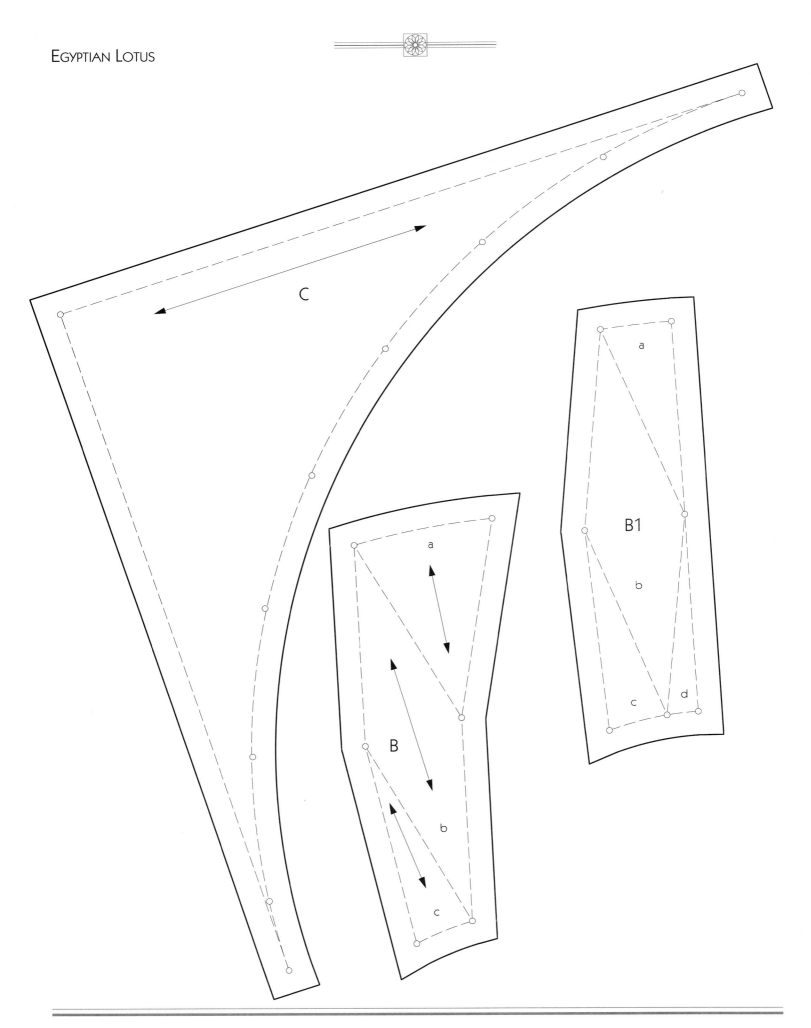

C

B1

a

b

c   d

B

a

b

c

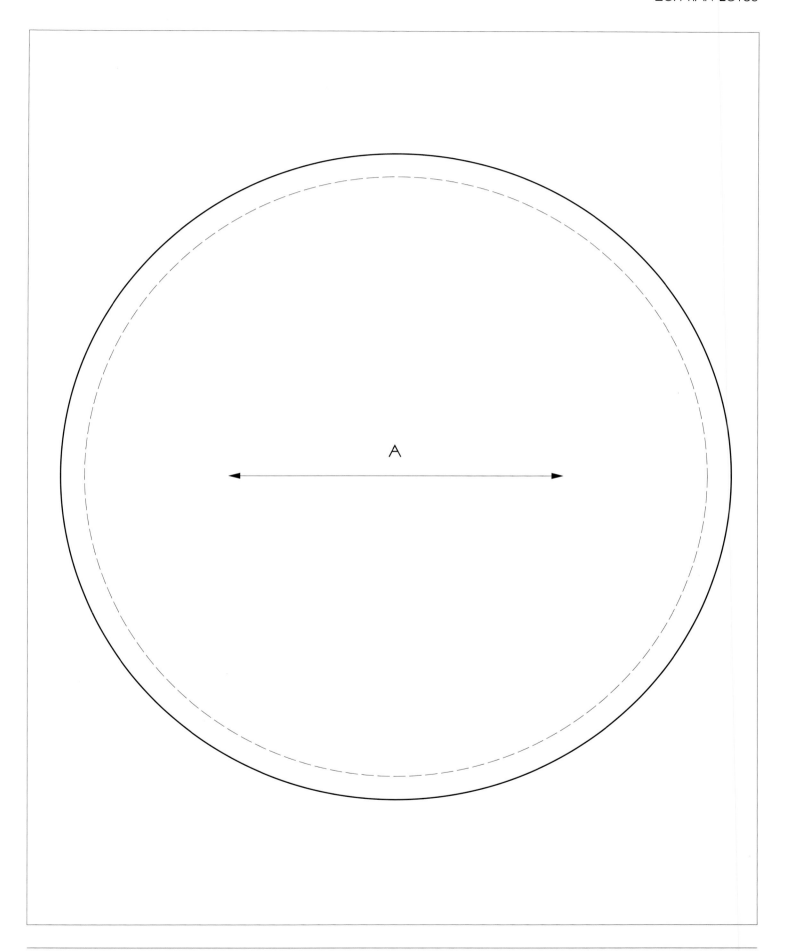

A

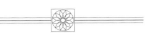

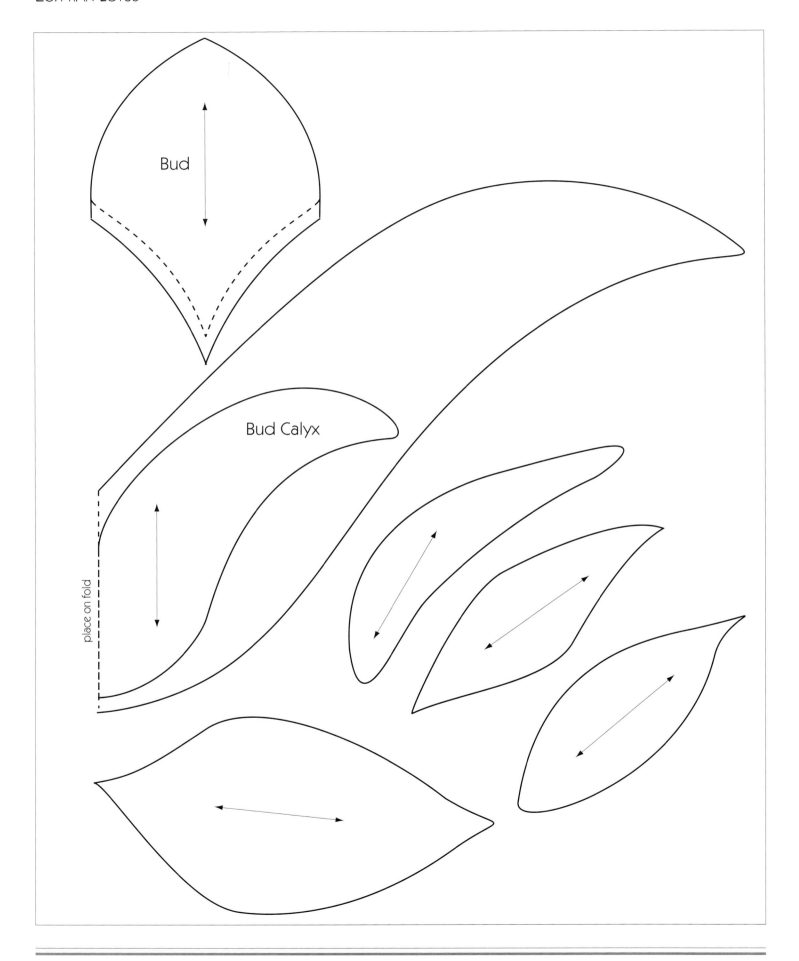

Bud

Bud Calyx

place on fold

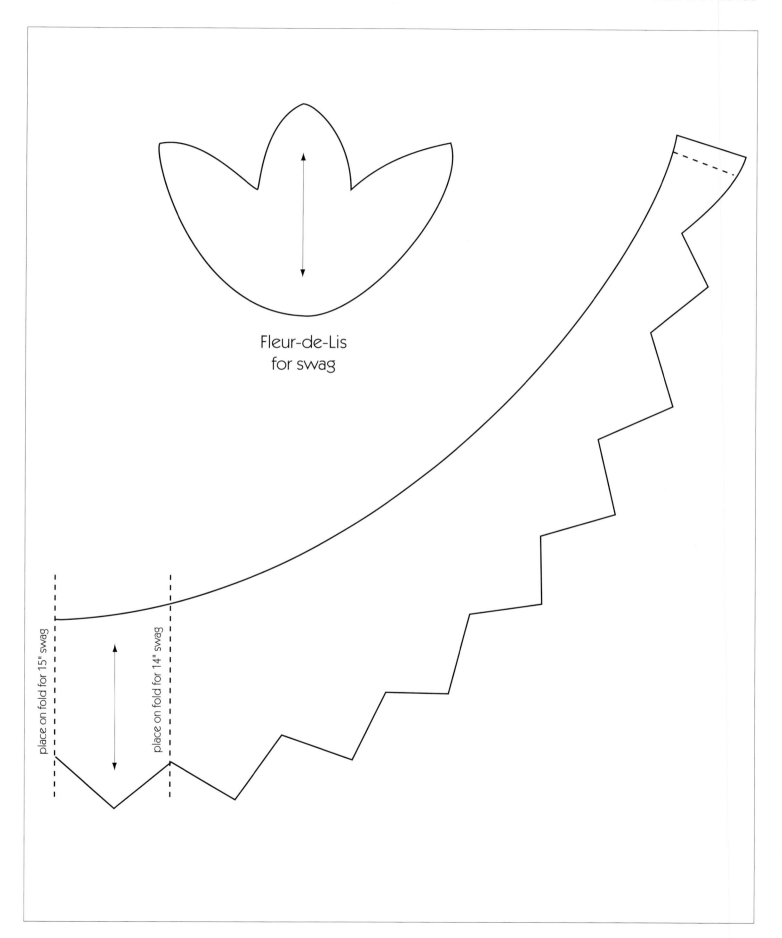

Fleur-de-Lis
for swag

place on fold for 15" swag

place on fold for 14" swag

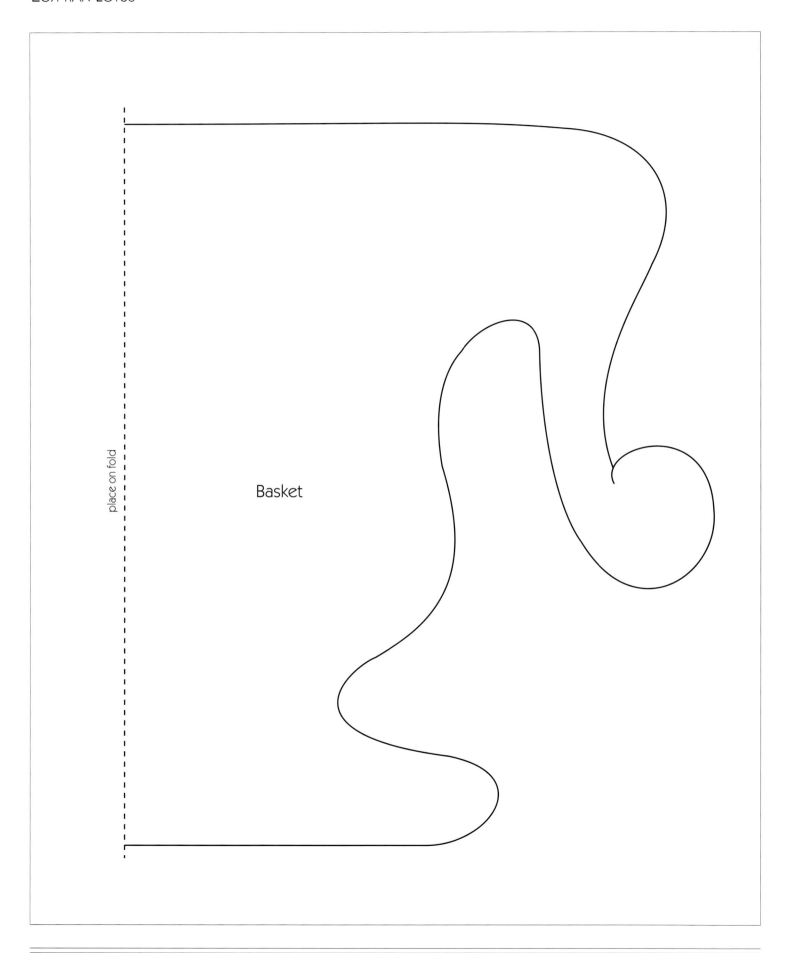

place on fold

Basket

Plate 5-19. Rattlesnake Variation. 34" x 34".
Sage, cream, and flax, all cotton. The tradtional Baby Bunting block
with a diagonal set. Unquilted.

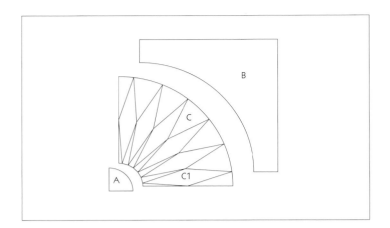

Fig. 5-70.

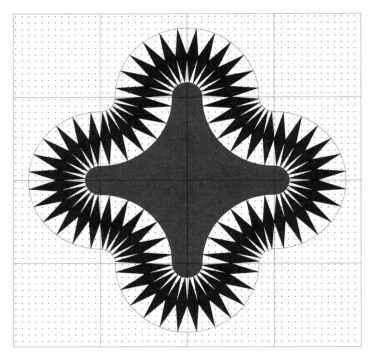

Fig. 5-71. Baby Bunting set.

Rattlesnake.

RATTLESNAKE VARIATION

Block size: This pattern is offered in three sizes 5¾", 8⅞", and
11¾".

The strips for the 5¾" block are cut
2½" for side a
1¼" for segment b
1¾" for side c

There are 7 striplates in each block.

Approximately 18 striplates can be cut from each 45" b strip.

The strips for the 8⅞" block are cut
2½" for side a
1¼" for segment b
1¾" for side c

There are 10 striplates in each block.

Approximately 10 striplates can be cut from each 45" b strip.

The strips for the 11¾" block are cut
3" for side a
1¼" for segment b
1¾" for side c

There are 10 striplates in each block.

Approximately 7 striplates can be cut from each 45" b strip.

Block Directions

• Piece the arcs, joining 7 striplate piece C's (5¾" block) or 10
striplate piece C's (8⅞" and 11¾" block) to make each arc.

• Stitch the corner units to piece B. *(Fig. 5-70)* Press the seams
toward piece B.

BABY BUNTING SET

Rattlesnake was designed to be set in the traditional Baby
Bunting Set. Baby Bunting requires 12 Rattlesnake blocks and
four plain corner blocks. The set size for the 5¾" block is 23".
The set size for the 8⅞" block is 35½" The set size for the 11¾"
block is 47". *(Fig. 5-71)*

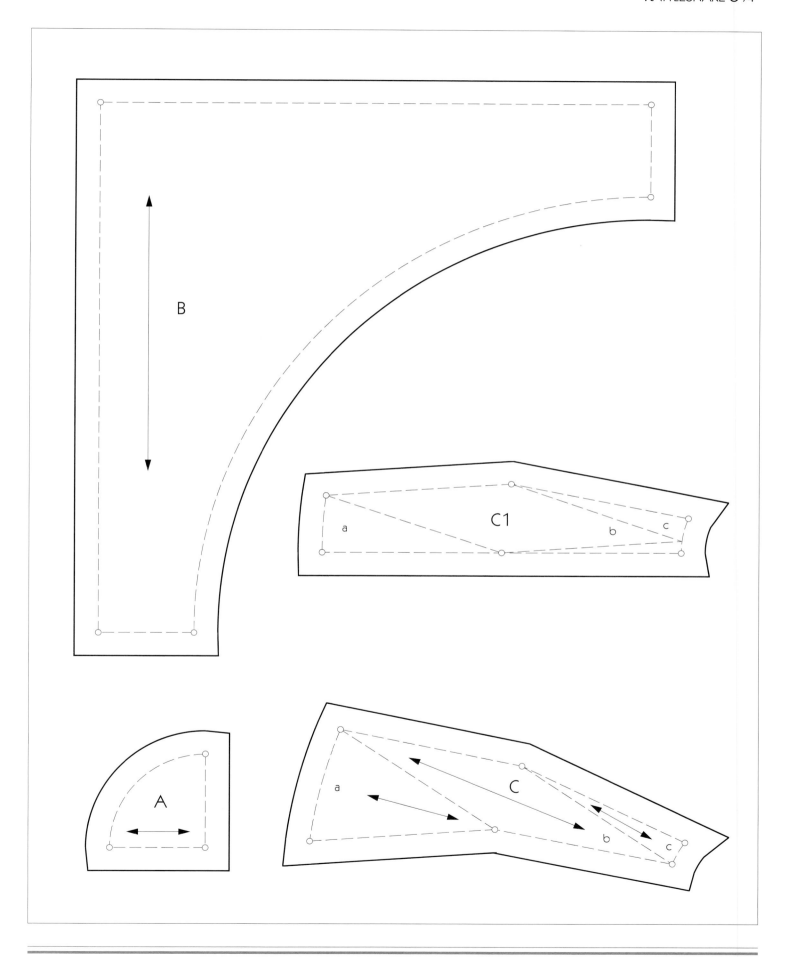

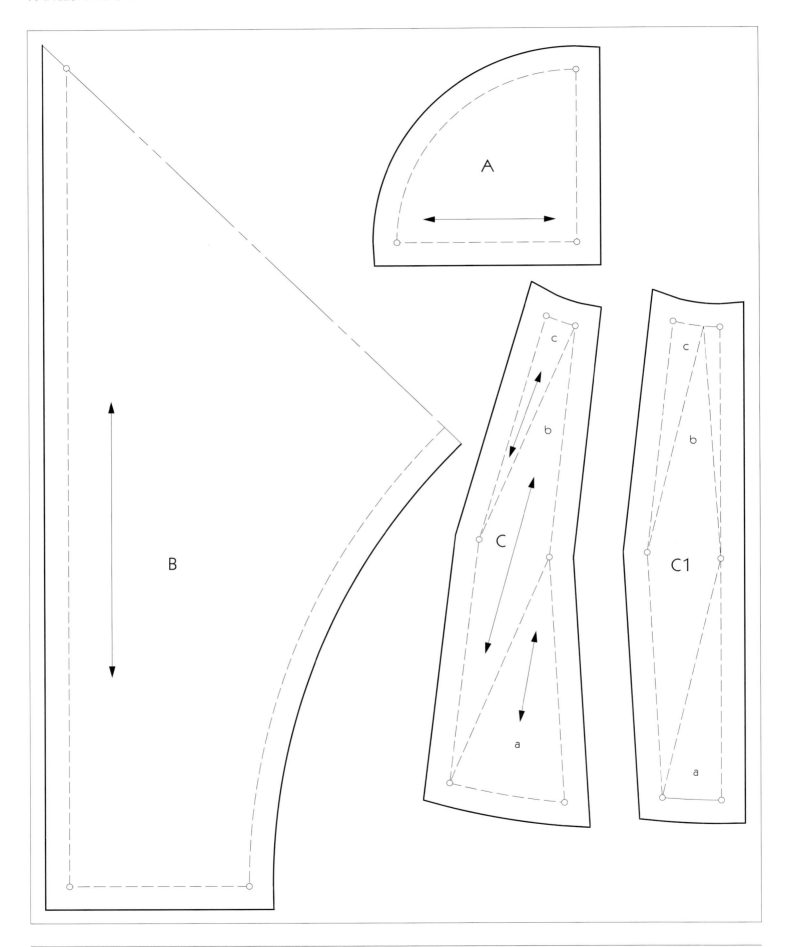

A

B

C

C1

a

b

c

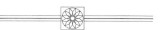

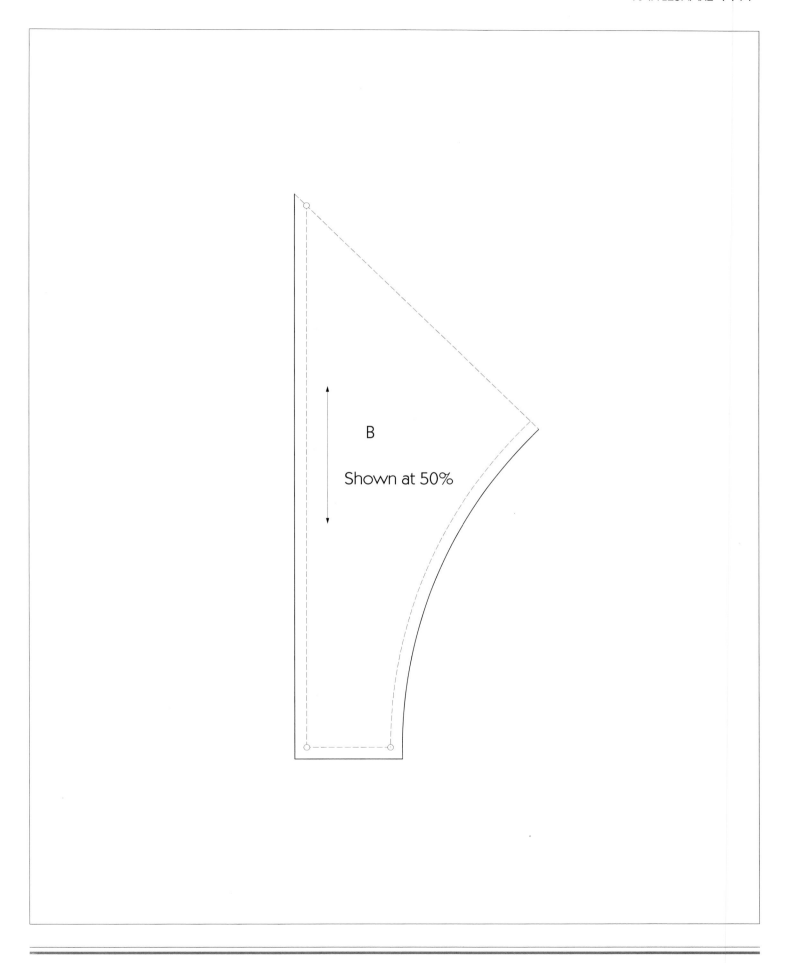

B

Shown at 50%

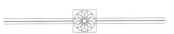

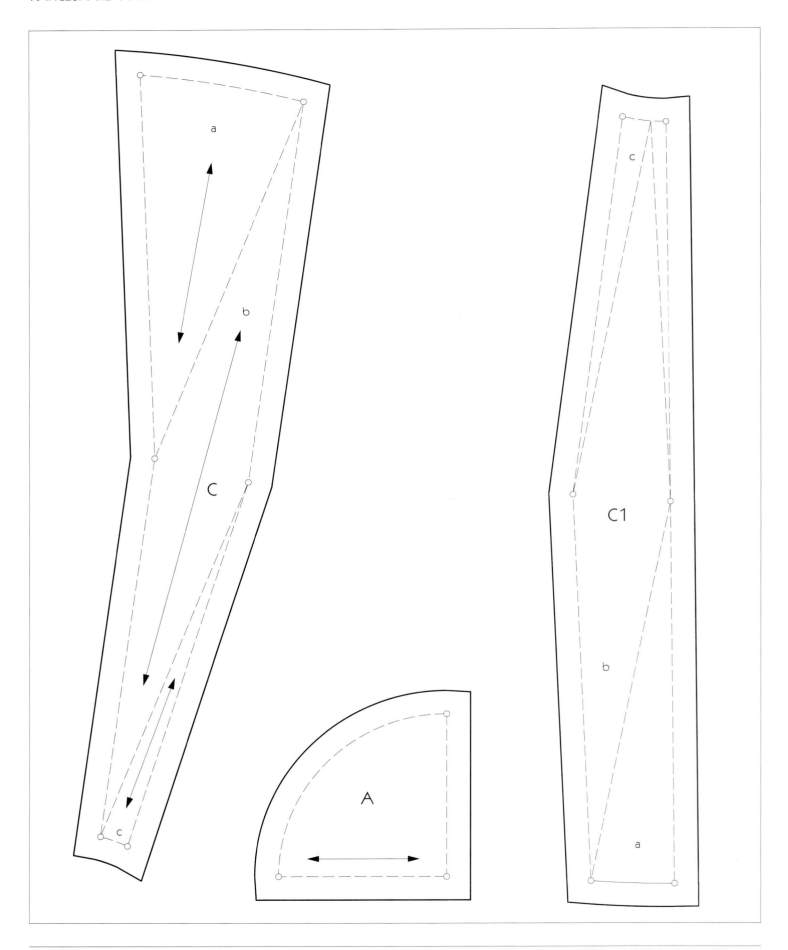

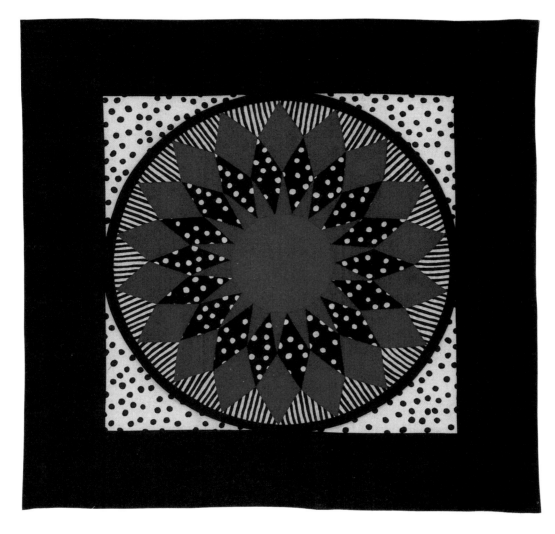

Plate 5-20. Centennial Sun. 17" x 17".
Black prints with red solid, all cottons. A single block with appliqué
bias trim. Bordered in solid black. Unquilted.

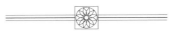

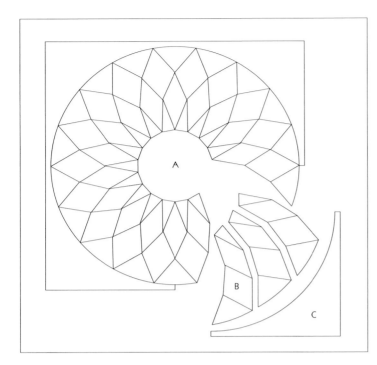

Fig. 5-72.

CENTENNIAL SUN
    Block size: 12"

    There are 18 striplates in each block.

    The strips are cut
        3" for side a
        1¾" for segment b
        1½" for segment c
        2" for side d

    Approximately 15 striplates can be cut from each set of four 45" strips.

    Please measure the pattern piece for strip b; it finishes slightly over 1¼" wide. Its exact measurement is 1⁵⁄₁₆", or half way between 1¼" and 1⅜". Cut a wide 1¾" strip to compensate for the discrepancy. To be exact, the cut should be at 1¹³⁄₁₆", or halfway between 1¾" and 1⅞".

<u>Block Directions</u>
- Join the strips in sets of four, a-b-c-d. Sets of four will conserve the most fabric.
- Piece the striplate circle by joining 18 piece B's.
- Join piece A and four piece C's to the striplate circle to complete the block. *(Fig. 5-72)*

Centennial Sun.

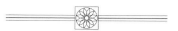

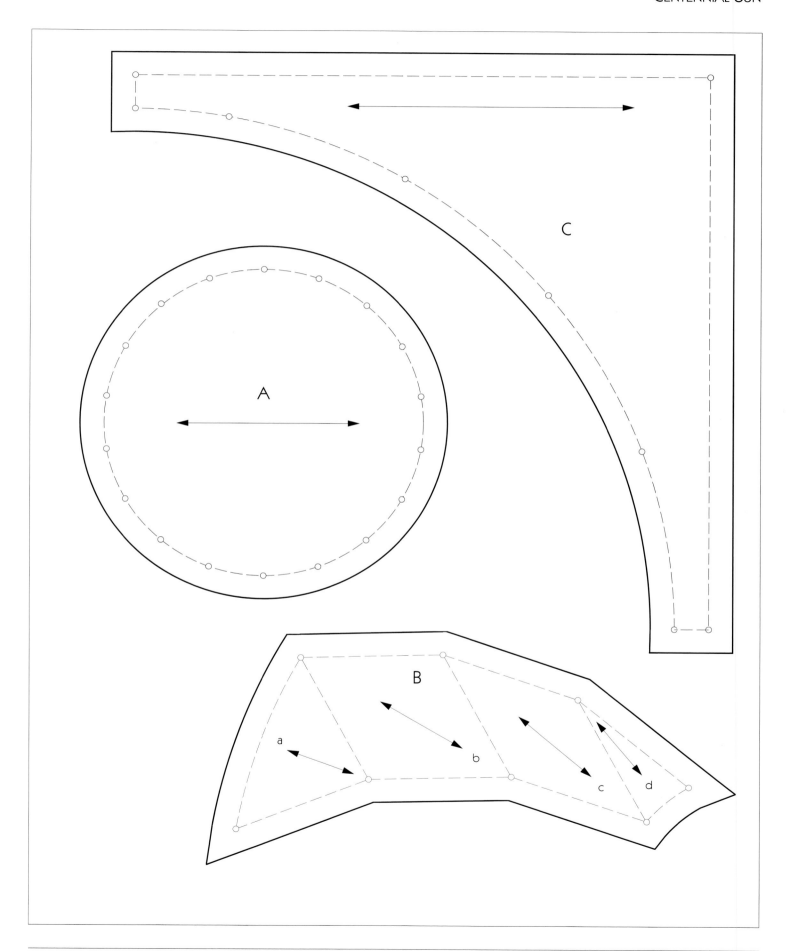

Plate 5-21. Susan's Sunflower. 17" x 17".
Gold prints and solid navy, all cotton. A single block with multiple
borders. Unquilted.

Plate 5-22. Susan's Sunflower. 9" x 9".
Red and white stripe with navy print. A single block with border. Note how the stripes are cut straight of grain to give the pinwheel effect. Unquilted.

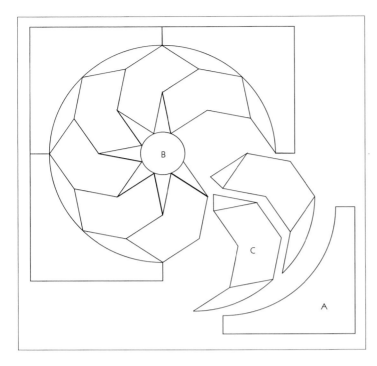

Fig. 5-73.

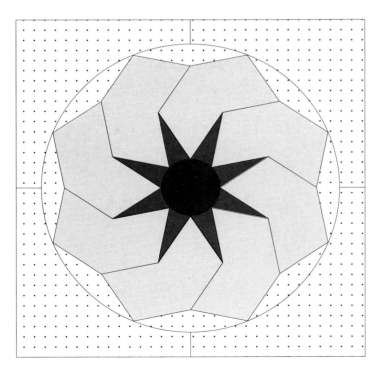

Susan's Sunflower.

SUSAN'S SUNFLOWER

Although this pattern requires only three strips, it is based on a four strip pattern and matches are sewn like a four piece striplate.

Block size: 9" and 12½"

There are eight striplates in each block.

The strips for the 9" block are cut

    1½" for side a

    3¼" for segment b

    1½" for side c

Approximately 11 striplates can be cut from each set of three 45" strips.

The strips for the 12½" block are cut

    1¾" for side a

    5" for segment b

    1½" for side c

Approximately 10 striplates can be cut from each set of four 45" strips.

Block Directions

- Join the strips in sets of three, a-b-c. Sets of three conserve the most of fabric.
- Piece the striplate circle by joining 8 piece C's.
- Join piece B and four piece A's to the striplate circle to complete the block. *(Fig. 5-73)*

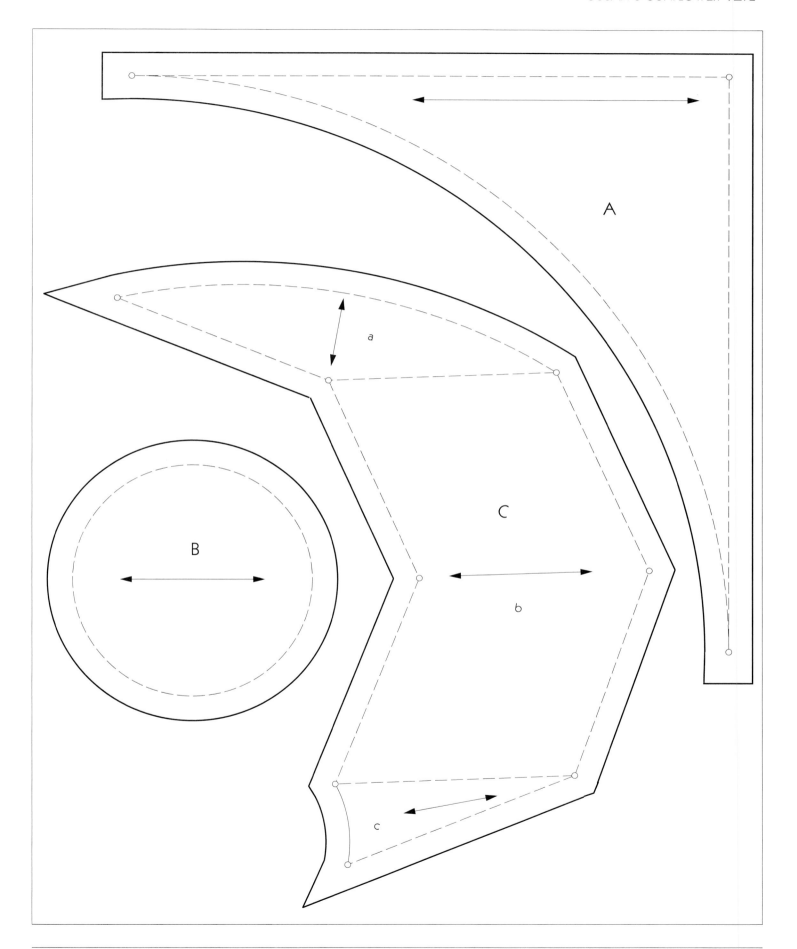

A

a

C

B

b

c

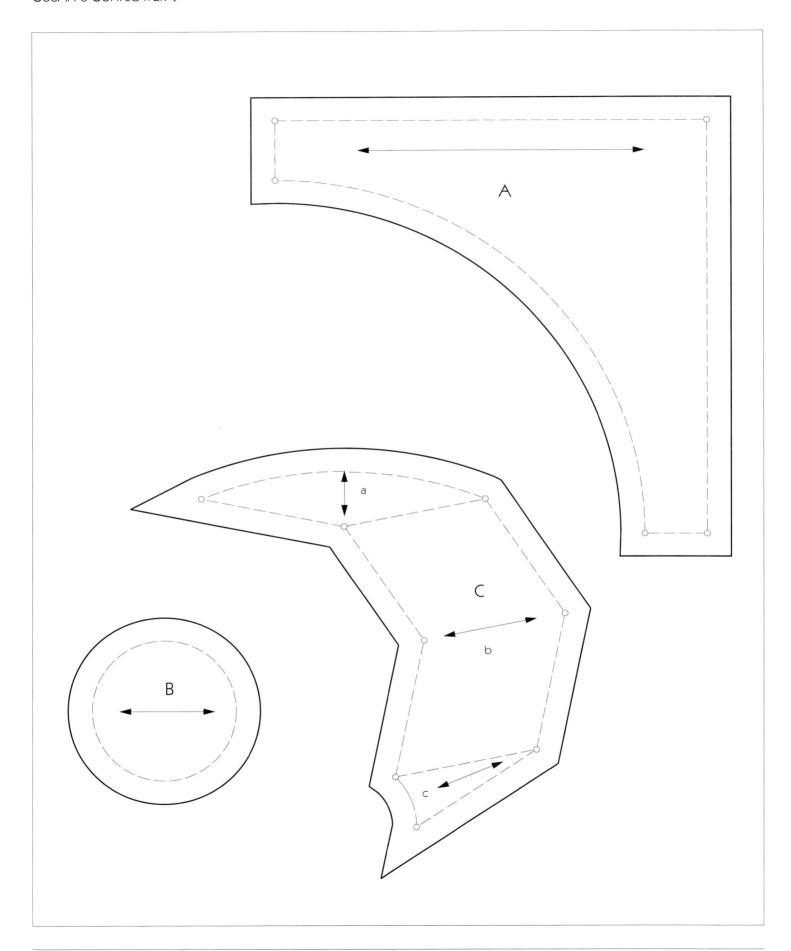

Plate 5-23. Sunny Splendor. 42½" x 42½".
Navy, tan, green, red, and pink, with striped printed border, all cottons. A single block with striped border. Unquilted.

Fig. 5-74.

Sunny Splendor.

SUNNY SPLENDOR

Sunny Splendor is a five-strip pattern, and is much like making a curved Lone Star. To make the pattern more interesting I have elongated the outer points of the sunflower. To compensate for the elongated points there is a single piece (a) sewn to the outer edge of every striplate piece.

Block size: 30"

There are eighteen striplates in each block.

The strips are cut

    5" for side a

    3" for segment b

    2⅝" for segment c

    1⅞" for segment d

    1½" for side e

Please measure the pattern piece for strip d; it finishes slightly over 1⅜" wide. Its exact measurement is 1⁷⁄₁₆", or half way between 1⅜" and 1½". Cut a wide 1⅞" strip to compensate for the discrepancy. To be exact the cut should be at 1¹⁵⁄₁₆", or halfway between 1⅞" and 2".

Approximately 10 striplates can be cut from each set of five 45" strips, when the strips are offset.

Block Directions

- Join the strips in sets of five, b-c-d-e-f. To make the best use of the fabric stagger the starts of the strips. Strip c should start 1" below strip b. Strip d 1" below c. Strips e and f should each be off set 1½" below the previous strip.
- Cut 18 striplates.
- Cut 18 piece a's and stitch them to the striplates.
- Piece the striplate circle by joining 18 piece a-f's.
- Join piece A and four piece B's to the striplate circle to complete the block. *(Fig. 5-74)*

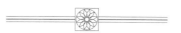

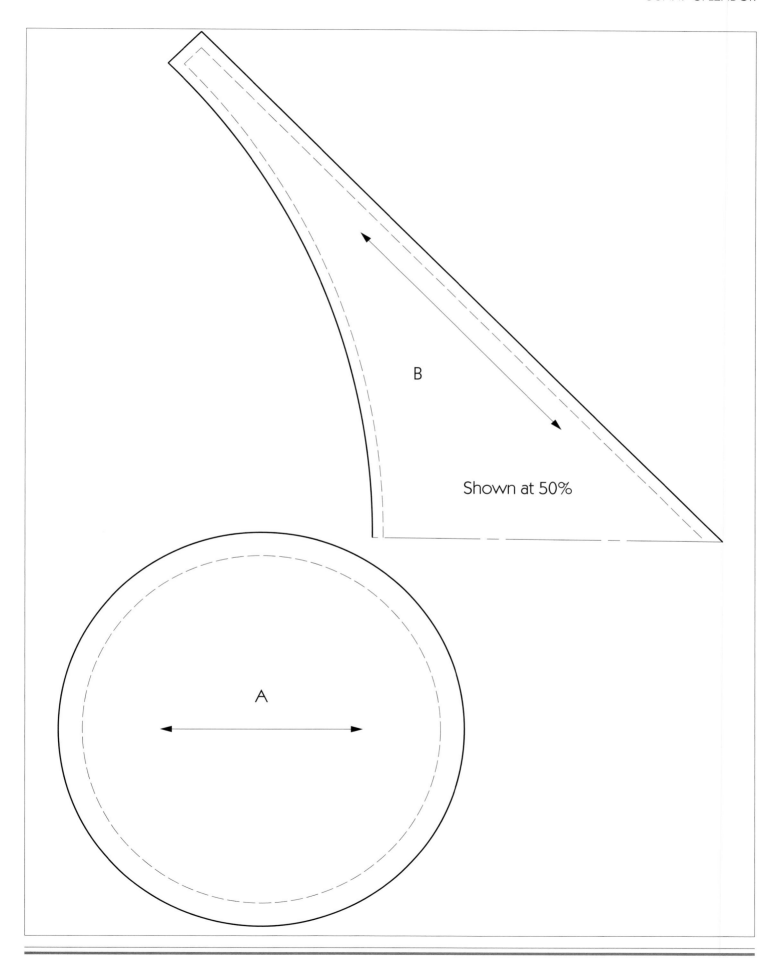

B

Shown at 50%

A

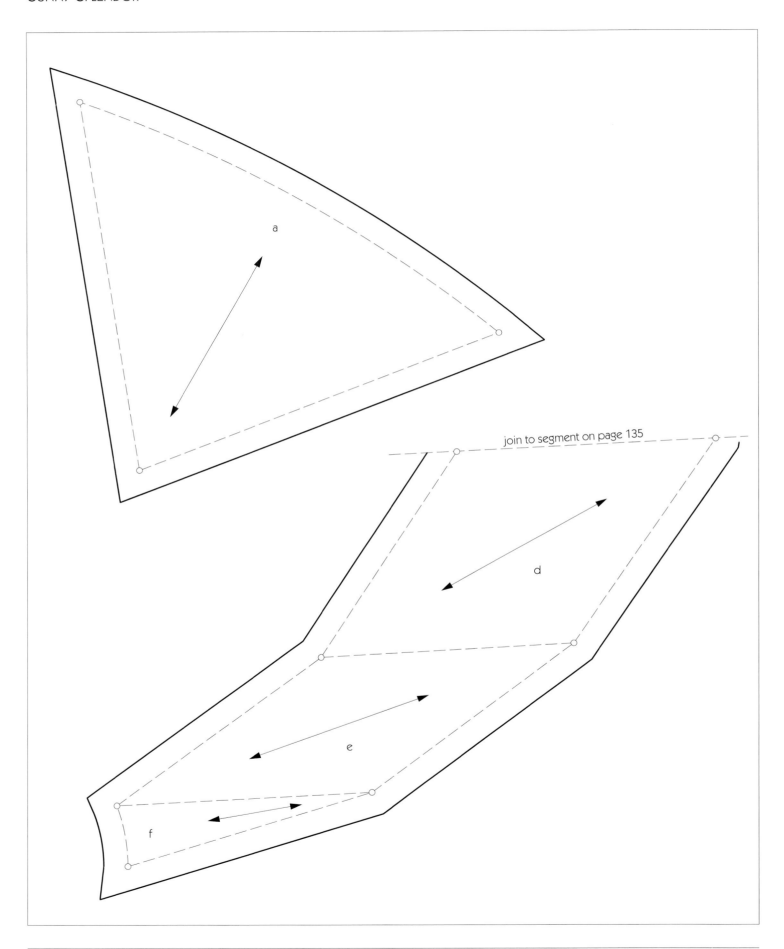

join to segment on page 135

a

d

e

f

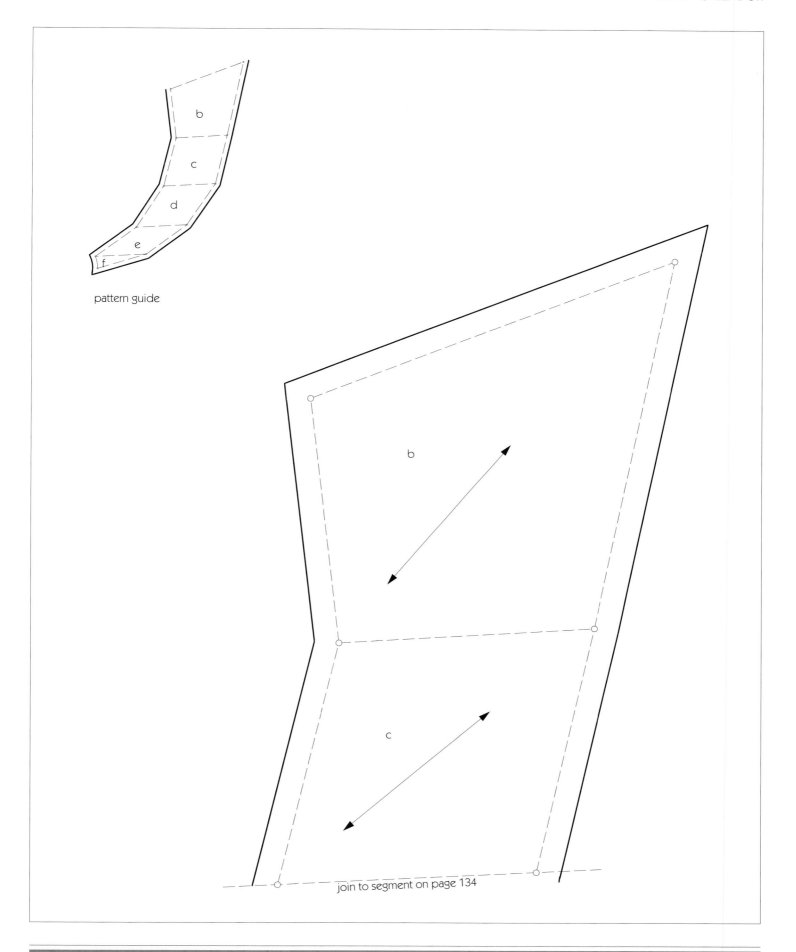

pattern guide

join to segment on page 134

Plate 5-24. Checkerboard Sunflower Variation. 18" x 18".
Cream, green, red, and gold, all cotton. A single block. Note the diamonds alternate between solid green and red and cream check. The
block has appliqué bias trim.

CHECKERBOARD SUNFLOWER VARIATION

The parallel edges of the striplate pieces make striplate patterns well suited for combining a number of strip piecing methods. Checkerboard Sunflower combines the strip pieced diamonds of the Lone Star pattern with the striplate patterns of Sunflower. The strip piecing is done in two steps. First the diamonds are cut and pieced. Then the completed diamonds are stitched to strips and the striplate pieces are cut. Although it may sound confusing, the technique is accurate and logical. This basic pattern was the starting point for my quilt DANDELION WINE.

Block size: 17"

There are 16 striplate pieces in each block.

The strips for the diamonds are cut 1½" for both sides of the diamonds.

There are two diamond sections in each diamond, or 32 in each block.

Approximately 20 diamond sections (B2) can be cut from a set of 45" strips.

The strips for the striplate piecing are cut
 4" for side a
 The completed diamonds are section b
  (for plain diamonds cut 2½" for piece b)
 3" for side c

Approximately 9 striplates can be cut from 45" strips.

Block Directions

• Join the strips for the diamonds. Use template B2 to mark and cut the diamonds. *(Fig. 5-75)*

• Stitch two piece B2's together to make a diamond. Make 16 diamonds for each block.

• Stitch the diamonds to strips a and c. Place the diamonds one after another, leave about ¼" to ⅜" between the diamonds. Work with only the three strips, a-diamonds-c. *(Fig. 5-76)*

• Using template B, line up the template to the diamonds, mark and cut the striplate pieces. Discard the unused halves of a and c. For the novice I would recommend working with only the three strips, a-diamonds-c. After working with the technique, it is possible to use the discarded halves of a and c to join to a new row of diamond pieces, but it will take a little practice to know how to correctly line up the half rows of a and c to the diamonds.

• Piece the striplate circle by joining 16 piece B's.

• Join piece A and four piece C's to the striplate circle to complete the block. *(Fig. 5-77)*

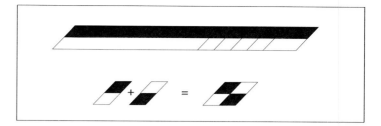

Fig. 5-75.

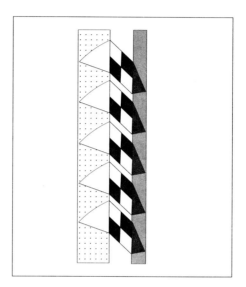

Fig. 5-76.

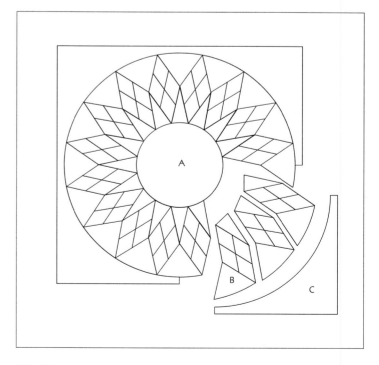

Fig. 5-77.

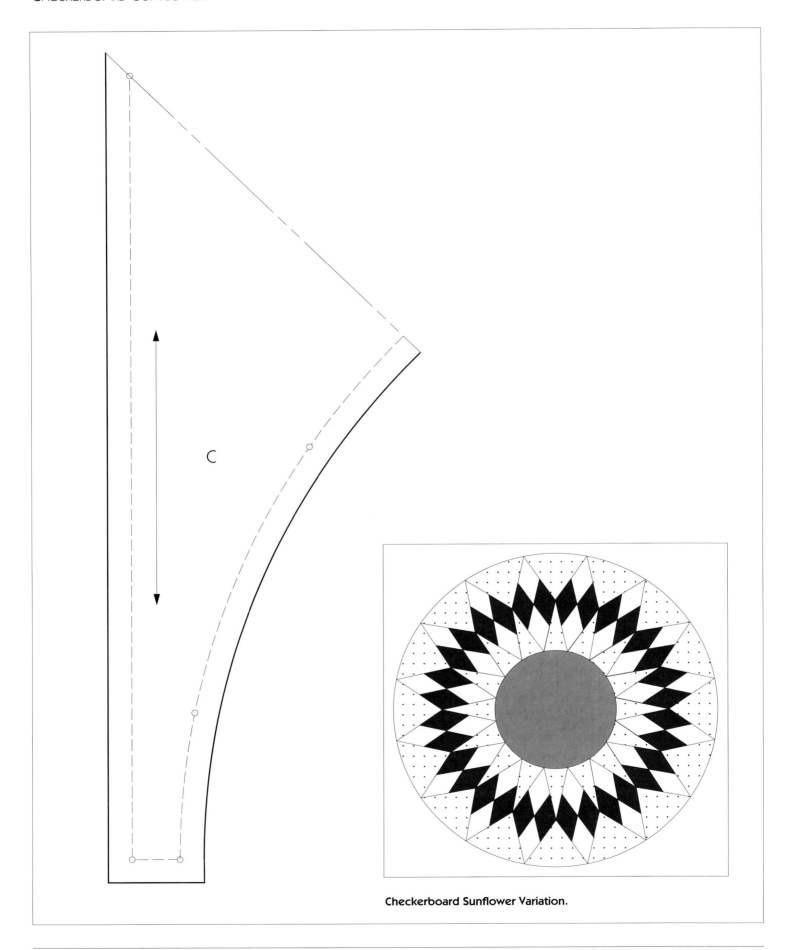

C

Checkerboard Sunflower Variation.

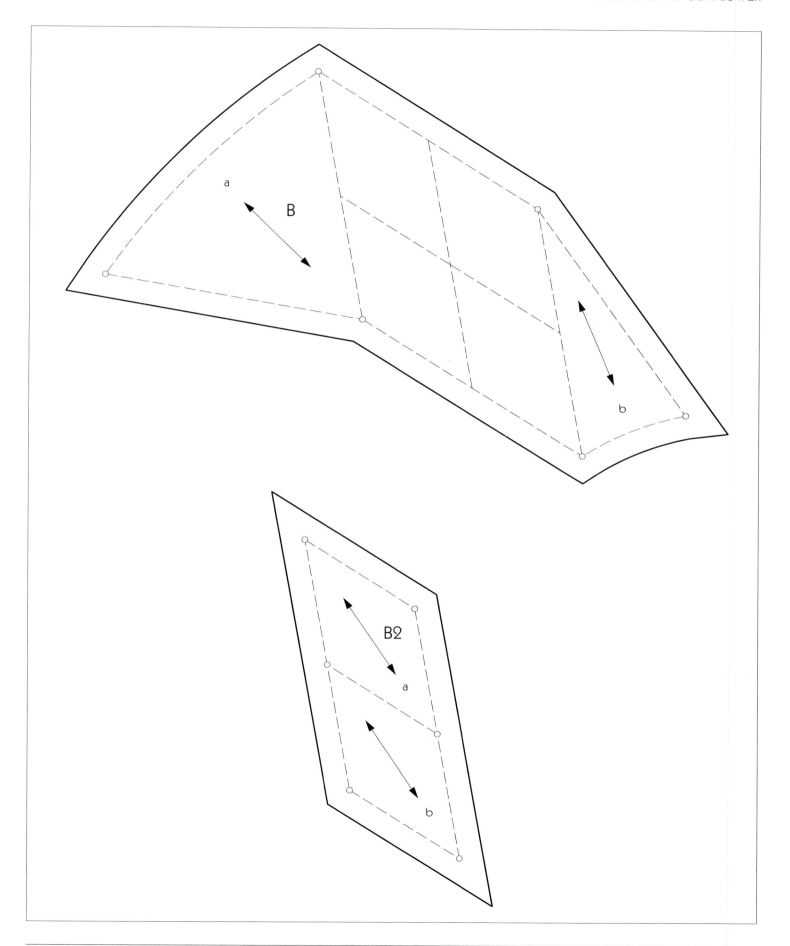

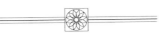

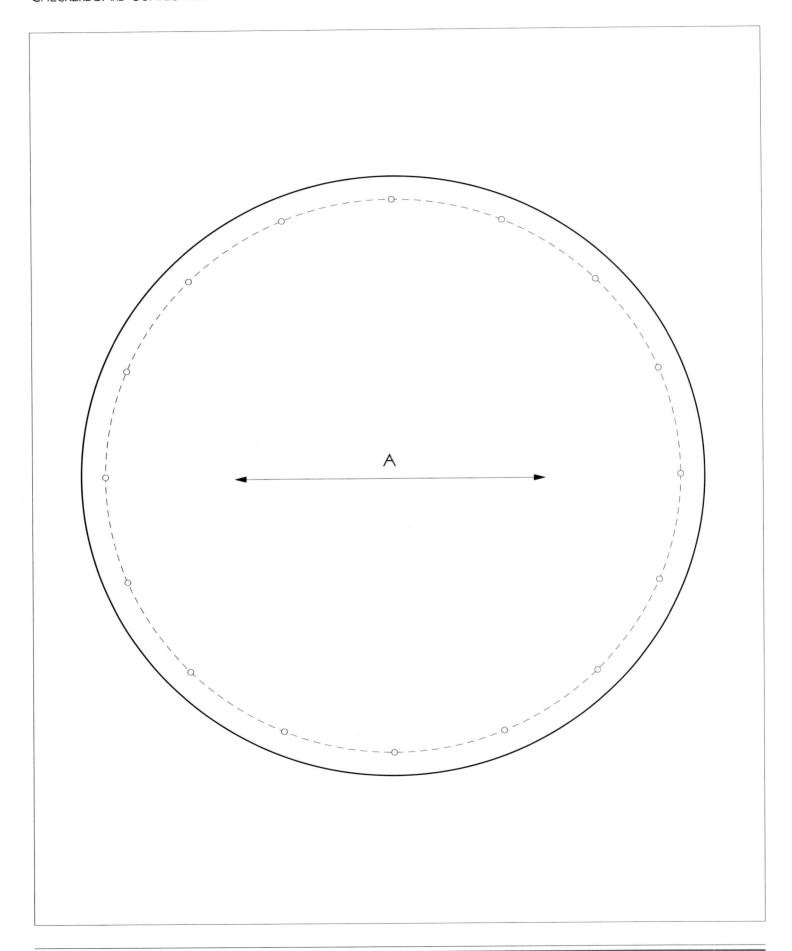

A

Plate 5-25. Georgetown Circle. 18" x18".
Blue and browns, all cotton. A single block, unquilted.

Fig. 5-78.

GEORGETOWN CIRCLE

Any parallel edge piece can be cut using striplate methods. Georgetown Circle is a good example. Previous patterns have used striplate templates for triangle pieces; Georgetown Circle use striplates for the triangles and curved rectangles.

Block size: 18"

There are four striplate piece templates for this pattern.

The strips for the inner ring B are cut

3" for side a.

2½" for side b.

There are eight striplate pieces in the circle.

Approximately 14 striplates can be cut along each 45" seam.

The strips for the second ring C are cut 4¾" for sides a and b. There are eight striplate pieces in the circle.

Approximately 20 striplate pieces can be cut along each 45" seam.

The strips for the third ring D are cut 5¾" for sides a and b. There are eight striplate pieces in the circle.

Approximately 16 striplate pieces can be cut along each 45" seam.

The strips for the outer ring E are cut

3" for side a.

2¼" for side b

There are 32 striplate pieces in the circle.

Approximately 16 striplate pieces can be cut along each 45" seam.

Block Directions

- Cut the required number of all striplate pieces.
- Join a single striplate of B, C, and D.
- Stitch four striplate E's together to make an arc. Stitch this arc to pieces B-C-D.
- Treat unit B-C-D-E as a single striplate and join eight units to make the circle. Use the same matching and stitching tehniques used with other striplates.
- Stitch one piece A and four piece F's to complete the block. (Fig. 5-78)

Georgetown Circle.

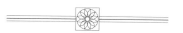

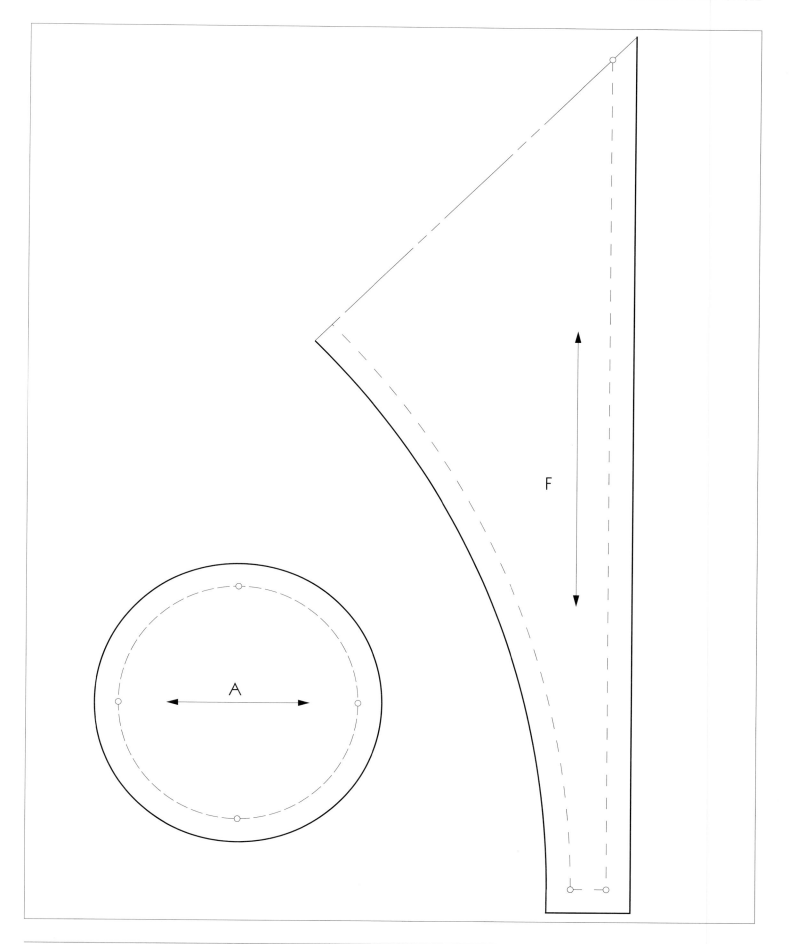

A

F

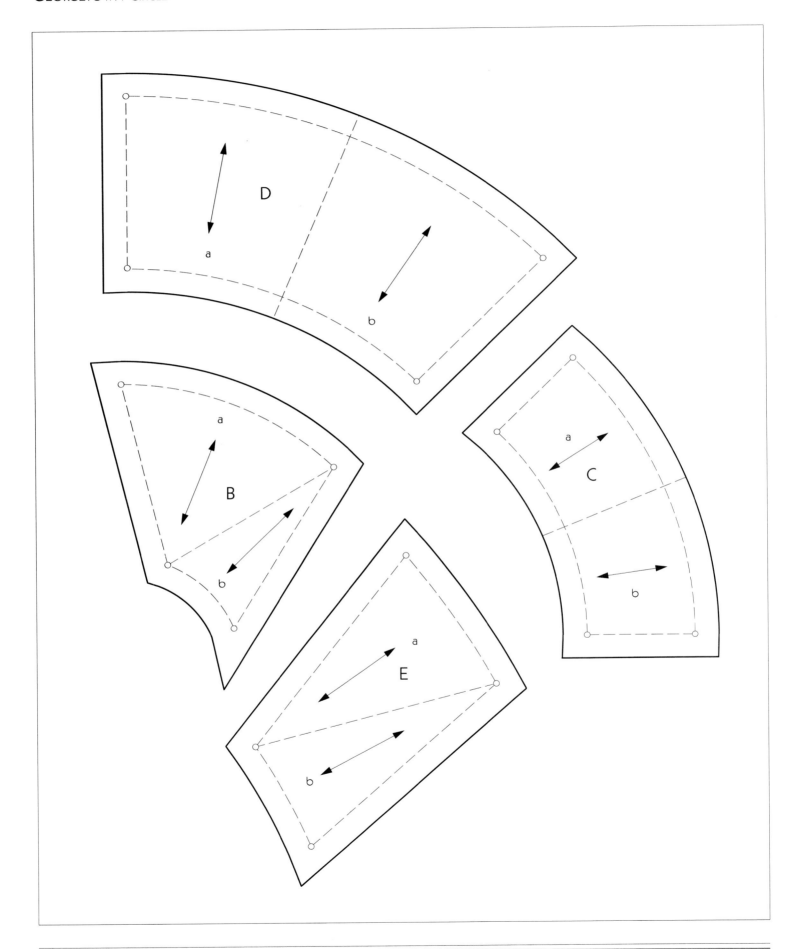

Plate 5-26. Farmer's Delight. 16" x16".
Browns, cream, and green, all cotton. A single block, unquilted.

Fig. 5-79.

FARMER'S DELIGHT

At 165 pieces this block could be a challenge using traditional methods. Striplate pieces reduce the number to 85. Farmer's Delight uses three striplate pieces and is constructed in units like Georgetown Circle.

Block size: 15½"

There are three striplate piece templates for this pattern.

The strips for the inner ring B are cut

3" for side a.

5" for side b.

There are 12 striplate pieces in the circle.

Approximately 10 striplates can be cut along each 45" seam.

The strips for the second ring C are cut 2¼" for sides a and b.

There are 36 striplate pieces in the circle.

Approximately 20 striplate pieces can be cut along each 45" seam.

The strips for the outer ring D are cut 2¼" for sides a and b.

There are 48 striplate pieces in the circle.

Approximately 20 striplate pieces can be cut along each 45" seam.

Block Directions

- Cut the required number of all striplate pieces.
- Stitch three striplate C's together to make an arc. Make 12 arcs. Stitch each arc to piece B.
- Stitch four striplate D's together to make an arc. Make 12 arcs. Stitch an arc to each B-C unit.
- Treat unit B-C-D as a single striplate and join 12 units to make the circle. Use the same matching and stitching techniques used with other striplates.
- Stitch one piece A and four piece E's to complete the block. (Fig. 5-79)

Farmer's Delight.

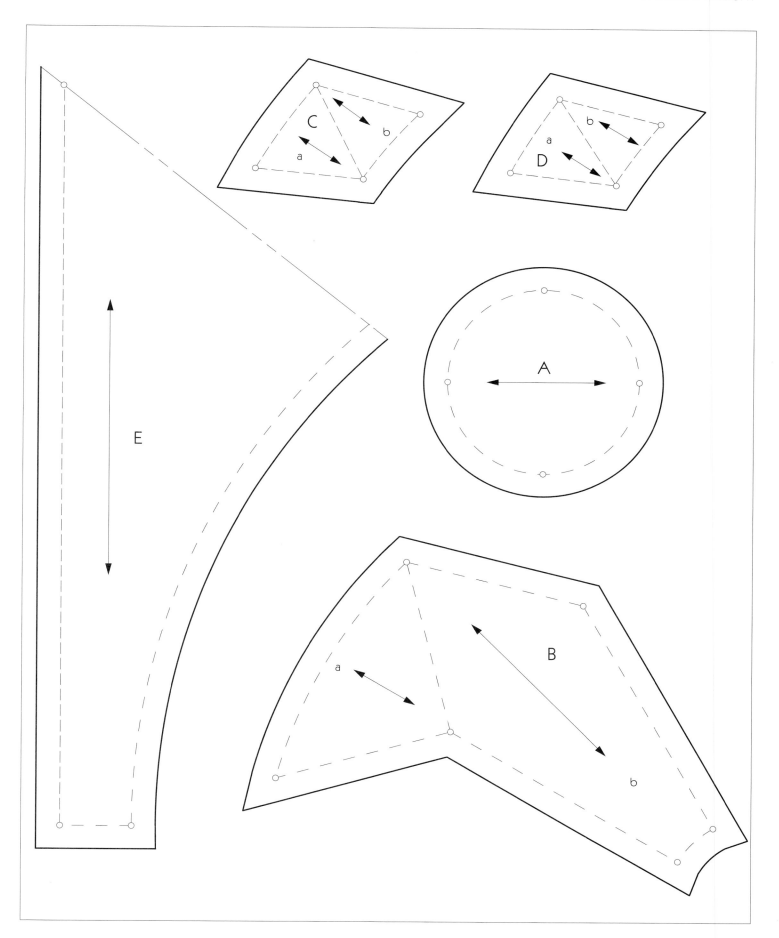

Plate 5-27. Winter Sun. 31" x 31".
Cream, red, and green, all cotton. This single block has an appliquéd
swag border. Unquilted.

Plate 5-28. Winter Sun Variation. 28" x 28".

Cream, black, and gold, with print border, all cotton. This version of
Winter Sun has only two rows of points, not three. It is a single block
bordered with a print strip, and a print cutout for the center of the sun.
Unquilted.

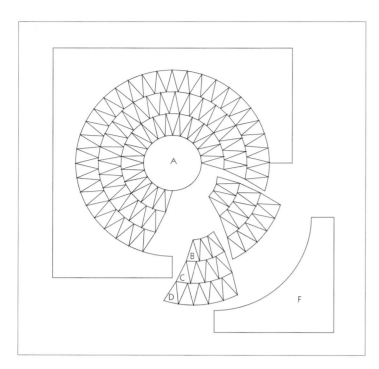

Fig. 5-80.

Winter Sun.

WINTER SUN

This block is my personal favorite. With a whopping 197 pieces per block, it sparkles like cut glass. The striplates reduce it to a mere 100 pieces, which is enough to keep the most avid piecer happy. Surprisingly the block goes together easily in eight big sections. The real trick is keeping the templates and pieces straight. B, C, and D are almost identical and mixing them can spell diaster. Like the two previous blocks, Winter Sun has multiple striplate templates and is constructed in units.

Block size: 18"

There are three striplate piece templates for this pattern.

The strips for the inner ring B are cut

2¼" for side a

2" for side b

There are 24 striplate pieces in the circle.

Approximately 18 striplates can be cut along each 45" seam.

The strips for the second ring C are cut 2¼" for sides a and b.
There are 32 striplate pieces in the circle.
Approximately 18 striplate pieces can be cut along each 45" seam.

The strips for the outer ring D are cut

2½" for side a

2¼" for side b

There are 40 striplate pieces in the circle.
Approximately 18 striplate pieces can be cut along each 45" seam.

Block Directions

- Cut the required number of all striplate pieces.
- Stitch three striplate B's together to make an arc. Make 8 arcs.
- Stitch four striplate C's together to make an arc. Make 8 arcs. Stitch each arc to piece B.
- Stitch five striplate D's together to make an arc. Make 8 arcs. Stitch an arc to each B-C unit.
- Treat unit B-C-D as a single striplate and join 8 units to make the circle. Use the same matching and stitching techniques used with other striplates.
- Stitch one piece A and four piece E's to complete the block. (Fig. 5-80)

WINTER SUN VARIATION

To paraphrase Shakespeare "One cannot have too much of a good thing!" I agree and have added one more ring to the Winter Sun. The result is a riveting display of triangles. This stunning block would make a great medallion for a quilt center. The addition is only slightly harder to construct than the original, but I don't recommend it for a beginner. The pattern piece for the fourth row has been included. This increases the number of pieces in the block to 148 (but it looks like 245 pieces). The fourth row of points is added around the basic three-layer Winter Sun. Cut both strips 2½" wide. The ring requires 48 pieces. There are six striplates in each arc. Make eight arcs. Stitch them to the eight arc units made in the basic steps. The fourth row increases the size of the circle to 18½". Because of space limitations I have not included the block background pattern. I suggest the background be at least 20" square. Use a compass to make the circle in the block background. Remember to draw the circle only 18" in diameter to include seam allowances.

Winter Sun Variation.

Plate 5-29. Winter Sun Variation. 33" x 33".
Cream, navy, and red with paisley border, all cotton. This version of
Winter Sun has four rows of points, not three. The single block is bor-
dered with a sawtooth border made with the striplate pattern from the
sashing in New York Beauty. The outer border is striped fabric.
Unquilted.

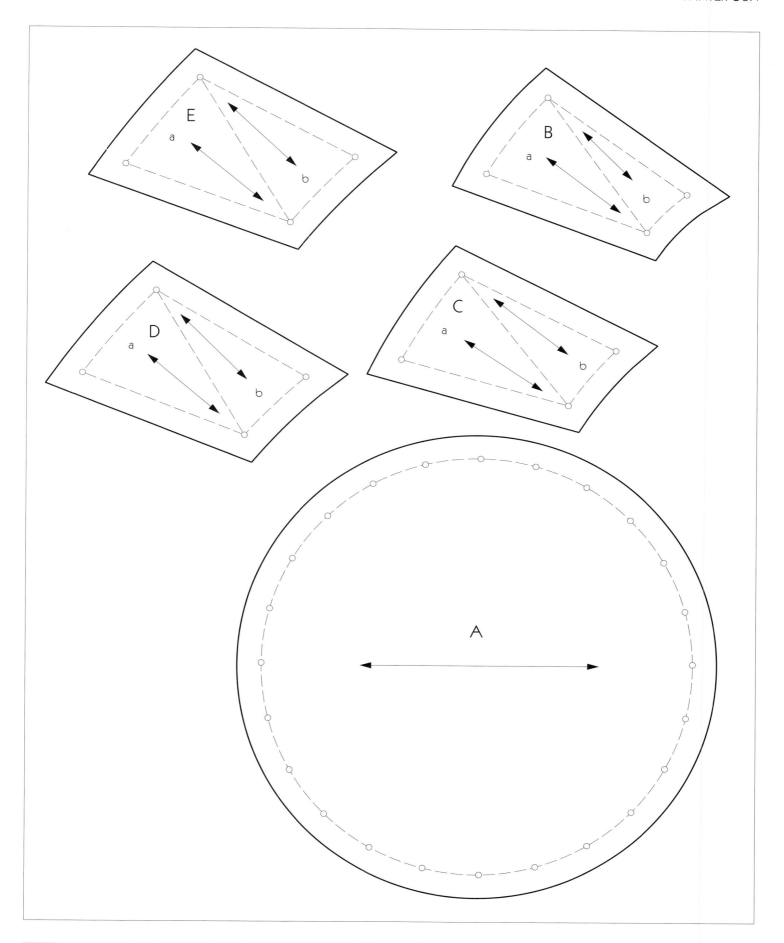

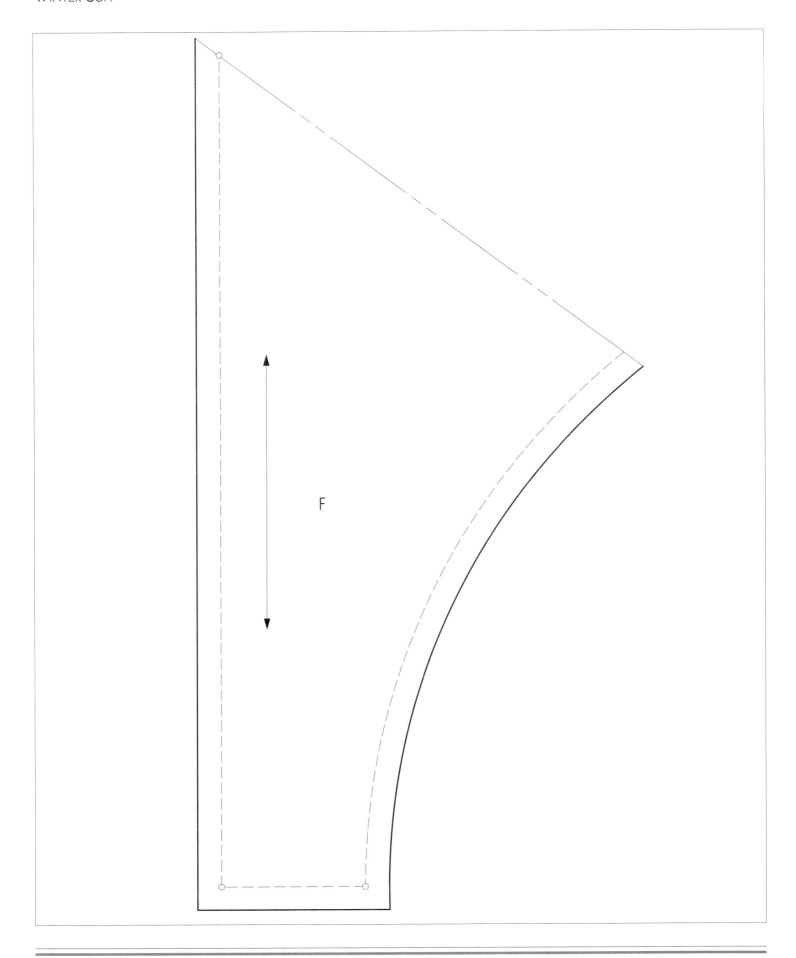

F

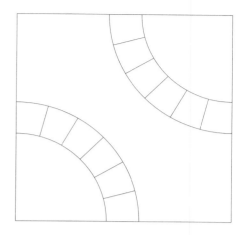

Fig. 6-3. Arcs in two corners.

Variations or Pattern Play

You can use a pattern just as it appears in the book or you may want to develop your own patterns based on striplate techniques. You might be surprised to realize that most variations don't require advanced drafting skills. You begin with the striplate arcs from the patterns and make easy alterations to the block backgrounds. You can think of the striplate as a building block. Any striplate template can be used for dozens of variations because every pattern, with the exception of Candy Dish and Friendship, is a based on a circle. That is why I chose to include a large selection of pattern styles, sizes, and complexities. Striplate patterns, especially multi-layer patterns, require trigonometry and careful drafting. The large selection gives you a varied choice of patterns without having to do the mathematics to design blocks. This way all the calculations are done and all you have to do is cut and sew the pieces.

Striplate blocks are based on whole circles, half circles, or quarter circles. There are five basic shapes for circle blocks. When you know the shapes and how they are designed, you can create your own patterns using the striplate arcs.

The five shapes are full circles (*Fig. 6-1*), quarter circles (*Fig. 6-2*), arcs in two corners (*Fig. 6-3*), arcs in four corners (*Fig. 6-4*), and Double Wedding Ring (*Fig. 6-5*).

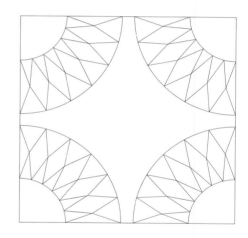

Fig. 6-4. Arcs in four corners.

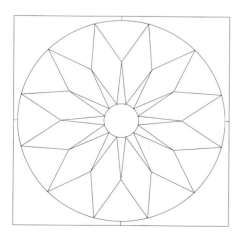

Fig. 6-1. Full circle.

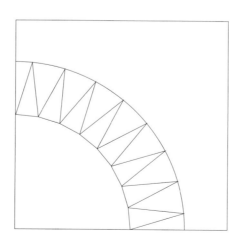

Fig. 6-2. Quarter circle.

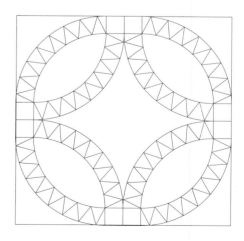

Fig. 6-5. Double Wedding Ring.

To manipulate the shapes you need to know the three basic parts of the patterns: the striplate arc, the block center, and the block background. *(Fig. 6-6)* Every circle pattern has those three pieces. This chapter will illustrate some variations of the basic patterns.

CIRCLE PATTERNS

Any arc pattern in this book can be made into a full circle by consolidating the partial circles. *(Fig. 6-7)* The circle blocks can be set alternating with plain blocks or sashed. You can also change the effect by changing the size of the block background. Or, the background block can be omitted and the circles hand appliquéd to the background in a random or very close set. Large block backgrounds can be pieced to make secondary patterns. It is common to see the background pieced with small corner squares or a LeMoyne Star. The effect can be changed again by adding pieced sashing to the blocks with piece backgrounds. *(Figs. 6-8 through 6-18)*

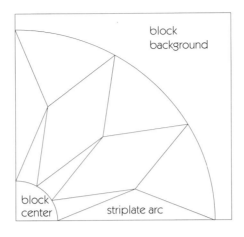

Fig. 6-6.

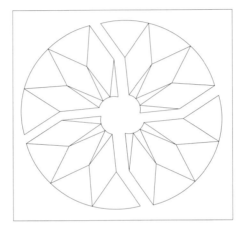

Fig. 6-7.

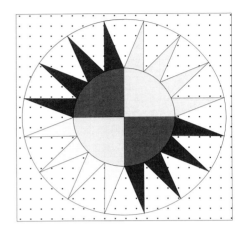

Fig. 6-8. Sunburst Variation.

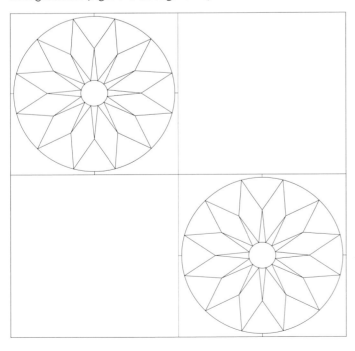

Fig. 6-9.

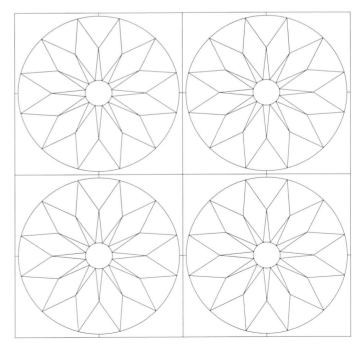

Fig. 6-10.

Fig. 6-11.

Fig. 6-12.

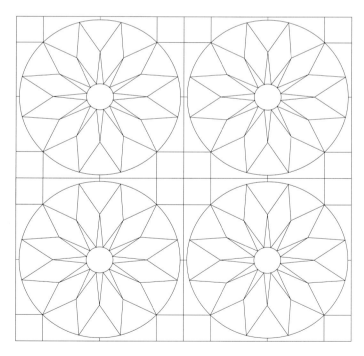

Fig. 6-13.

Fig. 6-14.

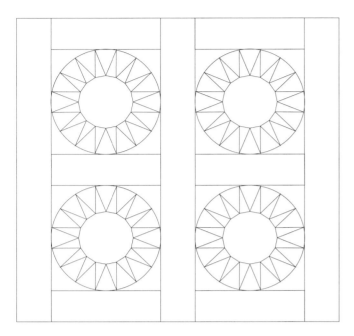

Fig. 6-15.

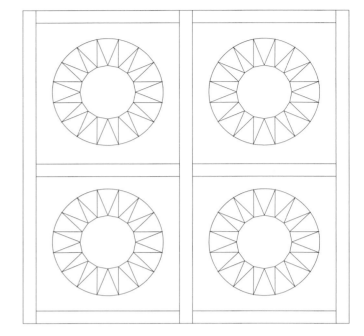

Fig. 6-16.

Fig. 6-17.

Fig. 6-18.

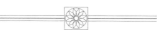

QUARTER-CIRCLE PATTERNS

Any circle or half-circle pattern with a number of points that can be divided by four can be used to make a quarter circle. *(Figs. 6-19 through 6-23)* Any Drunkard's Path set can be used for quarter-circle designs. With the addition of points to the basic Drunkard's Path, the variations have a common name of Sawthooth Drunkard's Path. Some variations would include: Baby Bunting, Wonder of the World, Drunkard's Path, Harvest Moon, Rob Peter to Pay Paul. Many of the variations depend on the reversing of colors in adjacent blocks. On some antiques the Sawtooth portions were all identical, with only the backgrounds changing; on other quilts both the Sawtooth and backgrounds changed. Three-color arcs like Rattlesnake can also be used in Drunkard's Path variations. The results are stunning. Surprisingly, very few antique quilts used three-color arcs.

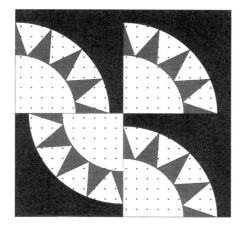

Fig. 6-20. Baby Bunting.

Fig. 6-21. Around the World.

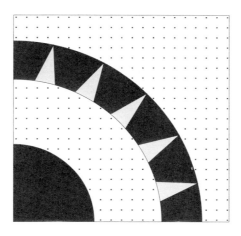

Fig. 6-22. Flo's Fan.

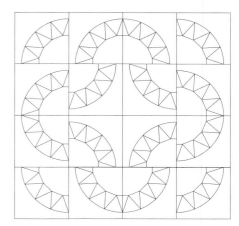

Fig. 6-23. Traditional Baby Bunting.

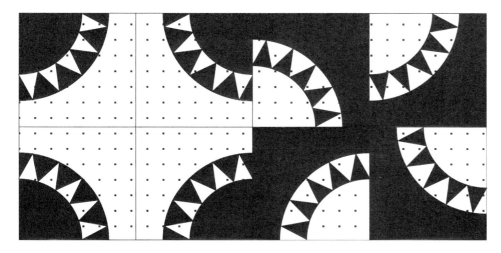

Fig. 6-19. Drunkard's Path Variation.

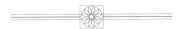

A unique variation of Drunkard's Path is used for Rattlesnake. *(Fig. 6-24)* On this block the background of Drunkard's Path and the center are the same measure so that when the blocks are joined a continuous line of Sawteeth is formed. *(Fig. 6-25)* This adjustment can be adapted to any block. The effect is dazzling when the block center and background are the same color. The Sawtooth sections appear to float and undulate over the quilt.

A variation called Snail Trail *(Fig. 6-29)*, Drunkard's Trail *(Fig. 6-27a and b)*, Marble Quilt *(Fig. 6-28)*, or Steeplechase *(Fig. 6-30)* combines two blocks from the previous pattern to make a square block with two arcs in the opposite corners. Again the background and center are equal measure. *(Fig. 6-26)* This variation works best when the center circle is quite large. When the center is too small the arcs touch or overlap.

All quarter-circle blocks can be altered by changing the arc ends. Changing the pieces cut in half by the arc ends is a simple variation. For example, most of the three-color striplate patterns divide the triangles in half. *(Fig. 6-31)* Changing the arc ends to divide the diamonds in half affects the overall look of the block. *(Fig. 6-32)*

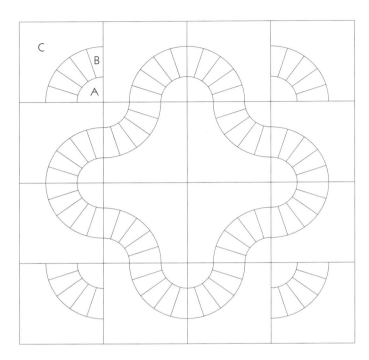

Fig. 6-24. Rattlesnake version of Baby Bunting.

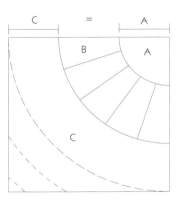

Fig. 6-25.

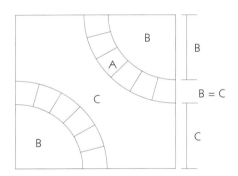

Fig. 6-26.

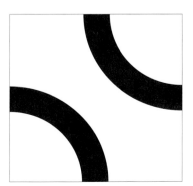

Fig. 6-27a. Drunkard's Trail.

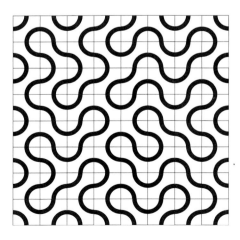

Fig. 6-27b. Drunkard's Trail.

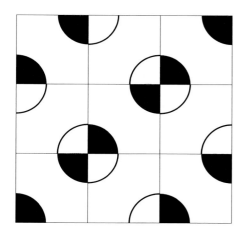

Fig. 6-28. Marble Quilt.

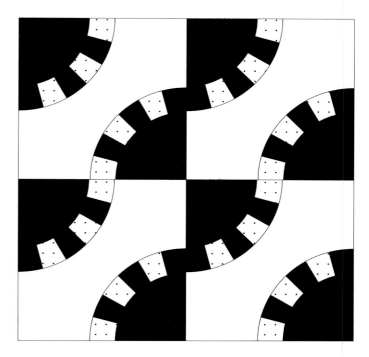

Fig. 6-29. Snake Trail.

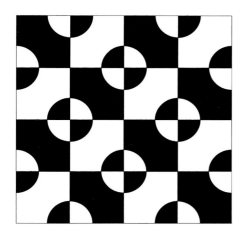

Fig. 6-30. Steeplechase.

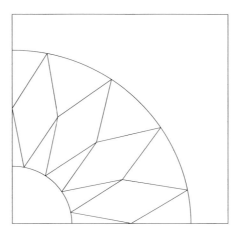

Fig. 6-31. Emphasize diamonds by dividing the triangles.

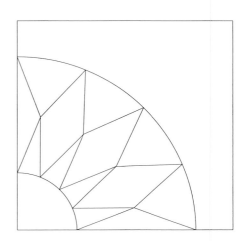

Fig. 6-32. Emphasize triangles by dividing the diamonds.

FOUR CORNER ARCS

Whig's Defeat, Grandmother's Engagement Ring, New York Beauty, Rocky Mountain Road, and Crown of Thorns are all based on a large block with an arc in each corner. These designs all depend on sashing or/and appliqué to make the pattern. As in all sashed patterns, the sashing can be altered by changing the width, color, and amount of piecing. There can be corner squares where the sashing joins or you can simply run the sashing across the quilt. The look of the basic block can be altered by changing the size of the background. The background can be a single piece or it can be a pieced pattern like a LeMoyne Star or four patch. The blocks can be set diagonally or straight. Blocks with pieced backgrounds include Suspension Bridge and Indian Summer. *(Figs. 6-33 through 6-38)*

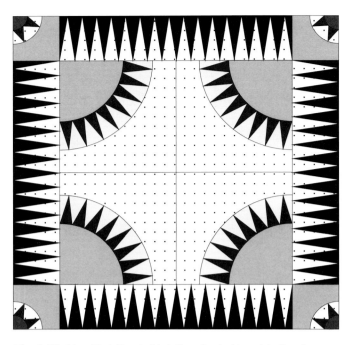

Fig. 6-34. New York Beauty Variation. Rocky Mountain Road.

Fig. 6-33.

Fig. 6-35. New York Beauty Variation.

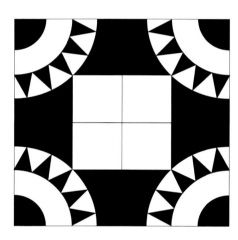

Fig. 6-36. Suspension Bridge.

Fig. 6-37. Indian Summer.

Fig. 6-38. Split Rail.

DOUBLE WEDDING RINGS

There are two types of Double Wedding Ring designs. One is made from true interlocking circles. *(Fig. 6-39)* The other is called Squashed Double Wedding Ring and is based on quarter-circle arcs. *(Fig. 6-40)* The squashed rings appear slightly square, but this design is easy to draft and allows for more creativity in design. All the Wedding Ring patterns in this book are the Squashed Rings. They are based on a block with arcs in four corners.

To design your own Double Wedding Ring block, start with the Whig's Defeat block. *(Fig. 6-41)* Alter the background to make the arcs touch or come very close to touching. *(Fig. 6-42)* That forms the center of the block. *(Fig. 6-43)* The circle centers will become the melon-shaped ellipse. *(Fig. 6-44)* Simply overlap two quarter circles until the curves touch and the two pieces form a square. The ellipse is formed in the overlapped areas of the circles. *(Fig. 6-45)* The connecting corners are always

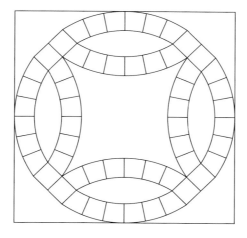

Fig. 6-39. Double Wedding Ring (circular version).

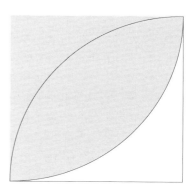

Fig. 6-44.

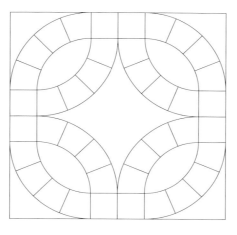

Fig. 6-40. Double Wedding Ring ("squashed" version).

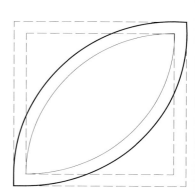

Fig. 6-45. This method even results in the correct seam allowances.

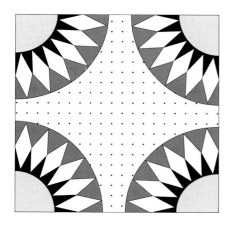

Fig. 6-41.

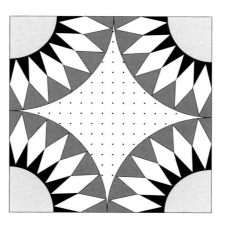

Fig. 6-42.

Fig. 6-43.

square. The square measures the width of two arcs and any space between them. (Fig. 6-46) The connecting square can be a single piece or it can be pieced as any other square. It could even be an appliqué. The choices are only limited by the size of the block and your imagination.

Double Wedding Ring quilts can be set three different ways. Two of the sets require pieced background blocks, but result in straight edges. (Figs. 6-47 and 48) For the stitching sequence for the traditional Double Wedding Ring design (Fig. 6-49), see Pickle Dish.

I hope I have given you some ideas that will help you design your own patterns. Striplate piecing can open a whole new area for quick piecing, and offers a way to accurately construct extremely complex blocks. Have fun and enjoy.

Fig. 6-46. Measurement for connecting corners.

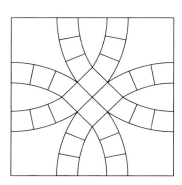

Fig. 6-47a.

Fig. 6-47b.

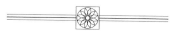

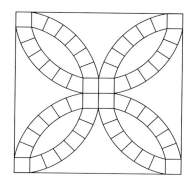

Fig. 6-48a.

Fig. 6-48b.

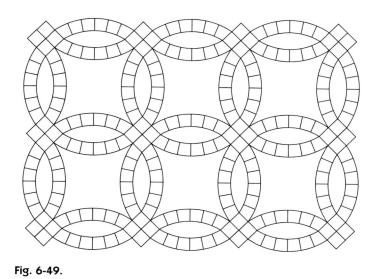

Fig. 6-49.

Bibliography

Beyer, Jinny. *Patchwork Portfolio*. McLean VA: EPM Publications, 1989.

————-. *The Quilter's Album of Blocks and Borders*. McLean, VA: EPM Publications, 1986.

————-. *The Art and Techinique of Creative Medallion Quilts*. McLean, VA: EPM Publications, 1982.

Bonesteel, Georgia. *Lap Quilting with Georgia Bonesteel*. Birmingham, AL: Oxmoor House, Inc., 1982.

Cory, Pepper. *Quilting Designs from Antique Quilts*. Lafayette, CA: C & T Publishing, 1987.

————. *Quilting Designs from the Amish*. Lafayette, CA: C & T Publishing, 1985.

Coyne Penders, Mary. *Color and Cloth*. Gualala, CA: The Quilt Digest Press, 1989.

Crow, Nancy. *Nancy Crow: Quilts and Influences*. Paducah, KY: The American Quilter's Society, 1989.

Fanning, Robbie, and Tony Fanning. *The Complete Book of Machine Quilting*. Radnor, PA: Chilton Book Company, 1980.

Fons, Marianne. *Fine Feathers: A Quilter's Guide to Customizing Traditional Feather Quilting Designs*. Lafayette, CA: C & T Publishing, 1990.

Goodmon Emery, Linda. *A Treasury of Quilting Designs*. Paducah, KY: American Quilter's Society, 1990.

Halgrimson, Jan, and Shirley Thompson. *Quilts – Start to Finish*. Edmonds, WA: St. Clair House, 1991.

Hallock, Anita. *Fast Patch, A Treasury of Strip Quilt Projects*. Radnor, PA: Chilton Book Company, 1989.

Hassel, Carla J. *Super Quilter II*. Des Moines, IA: Wallace-Homestead Book Company, 1982.

Hickey, Mary. *Angle Antics*. Bothell, WA: That Patchwork Place, 1991.

Hughes, Trudie. *Template-Free Quiltmaking*. Bothell, WA: That Patchwork Place, 1986.

James, Michael. *The Quiltmaker's Handbook: A Guide to Design and Construction*. Englewood Cliffs, NJ: Prentice-Hall, 1978.

Johnson-Srebro, Nancy. *Miniature to Masterpiece, Perfect Piecing Secrets from a Prizewinning Quiltmaker*. Columbia Crossroads, PA: RCW Publishing, 1990.

Lehman, Bonnie, and Judy Martin. *Taking the Math Out of Making Patchwork Quilts*. Wheatridge, CO: Moon Over the Mountain Publishing, 1981.

McCloskey, Marsha, and Nancy Martin. *A Dozen Variables*. Bothell, WA: That Patchwrok Place, 1987.

McClun, Diana, and Laura Nownes. *Quilts! Quilts! Quilts!* Gualala, CA: The Quilt Digest Press, 1988.

Mathieson, Judy. *Mariner's Compass, An American Quilt Classic*. Lafayette, CA: C & T Publishing, 1987.

Martin, Nancy J. *Back to Square One*. Bothell, WA: That Patchwork Place, 1988.

Nadelstern, Paula. *Color Designs in Patchwork*. New York, NY; Dover Publications, 1991.

Nownes, Laura. *Double Wedding Ring*. Gualala, CA: The Quilt Digest Press, 1990.

Poster, Donna. *Speed-Cut Quilts*. Radnor, PA: Chilton Book Company, 1989.

Risinger, Hettie. *Innovative Machine Patchwork Piecing*. New York, NY: Sterling Publishing Company, 1983.

Shirer, Marie. *Quilt Setting*. Wheatridge, CO: Moon Over the Mountain Publishing, 1989.

Thompson, Shirley. *Think Small*. Edmonds, WA: Powell Publications, 1990.

——. *Old-Time Quilting Designs*, 1988.

——. *Tried and True Favorite Old-Time Quilting Designs*, 1987.

——. *The Finishing Touch*, 1991.

——. *It's Not a Quilt Until It's Quilted*, 1984.

Wagner, Debra. *Teach Yourself Machine Piecing and Quilting*. Radnor, PA: Chilton Book Company, 1992.

Wolfrom, Joen. *The Magical Effects of Color*. Lafayette, CA: C & T Publishing, 1992.

Resources

AQS
P.O. Box 3290
Paducah, KY 42002-3290
800-626-5420
Books

Cabin Fever Calicoes
PO Box 550106
Atlanta, GA 05538

Send $2.50 for catalog. Fabrics, books, patterns, and notions.

The Cloth Cupboard
PO Box 2263
Boise, ID 83701

Send SASE with 50¢ postage for current product list. Fabrics and notions, most notably the ¹⁄₁₆" punch.

Keepsake Quilting
32 Dover Street
PO Box 1459
Meredith, NH 03252

Send $1.00 for catalog. Fabrics, books, patterns, and notions.

Quilting Books Unlimited
1158 Prairie
Aurora, IL 60506

Send $1.00 for current book list. A huge selection of books!

Quilts and Other Comforts
PO Box 94-231
Wheatridge, CO 80034

Fabrics, books, patterns, and notions.

∼American Quilter's Society∼
dedicated to publishing books for today's quilters

The following AQS publications are currently available:

- **Adapting Architectural Details for Quilts,** Carol Wagner, #2282: AQS, 1991, 88 pages, softbound, $12.95
- **American Beauties: Rose & Tulip Quilts,** Gwen Marston & Joe Cunningham, #1907: AQS, 1988, 96 pages, softbound, $14.95
- **America's Pictorial Quilts,** Caron L. Mosey, #1662: AQS, 1985, 112 pages, hardbound, $19.95
- **Appliqué Designs: My Mother Taught Me to Sew,** Faye Anderson, #2121: AQS, 1990, 80 pages, softbound, $12.95
- **Appliqué Patterns from Native American Beadwork Designs,** Dr. Joyce Mori, #3790: AQS, 1994, 96 pages, softbound, $14.95
- **Arkansas Quilts: Arkansas Warmth,** Arkansas Quilter's Guild, Inc., #1908: AQS, 1987, 144 pages, hardbound, $24.95
- **The Art of Hand Appliqué,** Laura Lee Fritz, #2122: AQS, 1990, 80 pages, softbound, $14.95
- **...Ask Helen More About Quilting Designs,** Helen Squire, #2099: AQS, 1990, 54 pages, 17 x 11, spiral-bound, $14.95
- **Award-Winning Quilts & Their Makers, Vol. I: The Best of AQS Shows – 1985-1987,** #2207: AQS, 1991, 232 pages, softbound, $24.95
- **Award-Winning Quilts & Their Makers, Vol. II: The Best of AQS Shows – 1988-1989,** #2354: AQS, 1992, 176 pages, softbound, $24.95
- **Award-Winning Quilts & Their Makers, Vol. III: The Best of AQS Shows – 1990-1991,** #3425: AQS, 1993, 180 pages, softbound, $24.95
- **Award-Winning Quilts & Their Makers, Vol. IV: The Best of AQS Shows – 1992-1993,** #3791: AQS, 1994, 180 pages, softbound, $24.95
- **Classic Basket Quilts,** Elizabeth Porter & Marianne Fons, #2208: AQS, 1991, 128 pages, softbound, $16.95
- **A Collection of Favorite Quilts,** Judy Florence, #2119: AQS, 1990, 136 pages, softbound, $18.95
- **Creative Machine Art,** Sharee Dawn Roberts, #2355: AQS, 1992, 142 pages, 9 x 9, softbound, $24.95
- **Dear Helen, Can You Tell Me?...All about Quilting Designs,** Helen Squire, #1820: AQS, 1987, 51 pages, 17 x 11, spiral-bound, $12.95
- **Double Wedding Ring Quilts: New Quilts from an Old Favorite,** #3870: AQS, 1994, 112 pages, softbound, $14.95
- **Dye Painting!,** Ann Johnston, #3399: AQS, 1992, 88 pages, softbound, $19.95
- **Dyeing & Overdyeing of Cotton Fabrics,** Judy Mercer Tescher, #2030: AQS, 1990, 54 pages, softbound, $9.95
- **Encyclopedia of Pieced Quilt Patterns,** compiled by Barbara Brackman, #3468: AQS, 1993, 552 pages, hardbound, $34.95
- **Flavor Quilts for Kids to Make: Complete Instructions for Teaching Children to Dye, Decorate & Sew Quilts,** Jennifer Amor, #2356: AQS, 1991, 120 pages, softbound, $12.95
- **From Basics to Binding: A Complete Guide to Making Quilts,** Karen Kay Buckley, #2381: AQS, 1992, 160 pages, softbound, $16.95
- **Fun & Fancy Machine Quiltmaking,** Lois Smith, #1982: AQS, 1989, 144 pages, softbound, $19.95
- **Gallery of American Quilts 1830-1991: Book III,** #3421: AQS, 1992, 128 pages, softbound, $19.95
- **The Grand Finale: A Quilter's Guide to Finishing Projects,** Linda Denner, #1924: AQS, 1988, 96 pages, softbound, $14.95
- **Heirloom Miniatures,** Tina M. Gravatt, #2097: AQS, 1990, 64 pages, softbound, $9.95
- **Infinite Stars,** Gayle Bong, #2283: AQS, 1992, 72 pages, softbound, $12.95
- **The Ins and Outs: Perfecting the Quilting Stitch,** Patricia J. Morris, #2120: AQS, 1990, 96 pages, softbound, $9.95
- **Irish Chain Quilts: A Workbook of Irish Chains & Related Patterns,** Joyce B. Peaden, #1906: AQS, 1988, 96 pages, softbound, $14.95
- **Jacobean Appliqué: Book I, "Exotica,"** Patricia B. Campbell & Mimi Ayars, Ph.D, #3784: AQS, 1993, 160 pages, softbound, $18.95
- **The Judge's Task: How Award-Winning Quilts Are Selected,** Patricia J. Morris, #3904: AQS, 1993, 128 pages, softbound, $19.95
- **The Log Cabin Returns to Kentucky: Quilts from the Pilgrim/Roy Collection,** Gerald Roy and Paul Pilgrim, #3329: AQS, 1992, 36 pages, 9 x 7, softbound, $12.95
- **Marbling Fabrics for Quilts: A Guide for Learning & Teaching,** Kathy Fawcett & Carol Shoaf, #2206: AQS, 1991, 72 pages, softbound, $12.95
- **More Projects and Patterns: A Second Collection of Favorite Quilts,** Judy Florence, #3330: AQS, 1992, 152 pages, softbound, $18.95
- **Nancy Crow: Quilts and Influences,** Nancy Crow, #1981: AQS, 1990, 256 pages, 9 x 12, hardcover, $29.95
- **Nancy Crow: Work in Transition,** Nancy Crow, #3331: AQS, 1992, 32 pages, 9 x 10, softbound, $12.95
- **New Jersey Quilts – 1777 to 1950: Contributions to an American Tradition,** The Heritage Quilt Project of New Jersey; text by Rachel Cochran, Rita Erickson, Natalie Hart & Barbara Schaffer, #3332: AQS, 1992, 256 pages, softbound, $29.95
- **No Dragons on My Quilt,** Jean Ray Laury with Ritva Laury & Lizabeth Laury, #2153: AQS, 1990, 52 pages, hardcover, $12.95
- **Oklahoma Heritage Quilts,** Oklahoma Quilt Heritage Project #2032: AQS, 1990, 144 pages, softbound, $19.95
- **Old Favorites in Miniature,** Tina Gravatt #3469: AQS, 1993, 104 pages, softbound, $15.95
- **A Patchwork of Pieces: An Anthology of Early Quilt Stories 1845-1940,** compiled by Cuesta Ray Benberry and Carol Pinney Crabb, #3333: AQS, 1993, 360 pages, 5½ x 8½, softbound, $14.95
- **Quilt Groups Today: Who They Are, Where They Meet, What They Do, and How to Contact Them – A Complete Guide for 1992-1993,** #3308: AQS, 1992, 336 pages, softbound, $14.95
- **Quilt Registry,** Lynne Fritz, #2380: AQS, 1992, 80 pages, hardbound, $9.95
- **Quilting Patterns from Native American Designs,** Dr. Joyce Mori, #3467: AQS, 1993, 80 pages, softbound, $12.95
- **Quilting with Style: Principles for Great Pattern Design,** Gwen Marston & Joe Cunningham, #3470: AQS, 1993, 192 pages, 9 x 12, hardbound, $24.95
- **Quiltmaker's Guide: Basics & Beyond,** Carol Doak, #2284: AQS, 1992, 208 pages, softbound, $19.95
- **Quilts: Old & New, A Similar View,** Paul D. Pilgrim and Gerald E. Roy, #3715: AQS, 1993, 40 pages, softbound, $12.95
- **Quilts: The Permanent Collection – MAQS,** #2257: AQS, 1991, 100 pages, 10 x 6½, softbound, $9.95
- **Seasons of the Heart & Home: Quilts for a Winter's Day,** Jan Patek, #3796: AQS, 1993, 160 pages, softbound, $18.95
- **Seasons of the Heart & Home: Quilts for Summer Days,** Jan Patek, #3761: AQS, 1993, 160 pages, softbound, $18.95
- **Sensational Scrap Quilts,** Darra Duffy Williamson, #2357: AQS, 1992, 152 pages, softbound, $24.95
- **Sets & Borders,** Gwen Marston & Joe Cunningham, #1821: AQS, 1987, 104 pages, softbound, $14.95
- **Show Me Helen...How to Use Quilting Designs,** Helen Squire, #3375: AQS, 1993, 155 pages, softbound, $15.95
- **Somewhere in Between: Quilts and Quilters of Illinois,** Rita Barrow Barber, #1790: AQS, 1986, 78 pages, softbound, $14.95
- **Spike & Zola: Patterns for Laughter...and Appliqué, Painting, or Stenciling,** Donna French Collins, #3794: AQS, 1993, 72 pages, softbound, $9.95
- **Stenciled Quilts for Christmas,** Marie Monteith Sturmer, #2098: AQS, 1990, 104 pages, softbound, $14.95
- **Three-Dimensional Appliqué and Embroidery Embellishment: Techniques for Today's Album Quilt,** Anita Shackelford, #3788: AQS, 1993, 152 pages, 9 x 12, hardbound, $24.95
- **A Treasury of Quilting Designs,** Linda Goodmon Emery, #2029: AQS, 1990, 80 pages, 14 x 11, spiral-bound, $14.95
- **Tricks with Chintz: Using Large Prints to Add New Magic to Traditional Quilt Blocks,** Nancy S. Breland, #3847: AQS, 1994, 96 pages, softbound, $14.95
- **Wonderful Wearables: A Celebration of Creative Clothing,** Virginia Avery, #2286: AQS, 1991, 184 pages, softbound, $24.95

These books can be found in local bookstores and quilt shops. If you are unable to locate a title in your area, you can order by mail from AQS, P.O. Box 3290, Paducah, KY 42002-3290. Please add $1 for the first book and 40¢ for each additional one to cover postage and handling. (International orders please add $1.50 for the first book and $1 for each additional one.)